CW0051743S

Reminiscences 1808-1815 Under Wellington

The Peninsular and Waterloo Memoirs of William Hay

William Hay with New Introduction, Notes and Commentary by Andrew Bamford

Helion & Company Limited

Helion & Company Limited
26 Willow Road
Solihull
West Midlands
B91 1UE
England
Tel. 0121 705 3393
Fax 0121 711 4075
Email: info@helion.co.uk
Website: www.helion.co.uk
Twitter: @helionbooks
Visit our blog at http://blog.helion.co.uk/

Published by Helion & Company 2017
Designed and typeset by Mach 3 Solutions Ltd (www.mach3solutions.co.uk)
Cover designed by Paul Hewitt, Battlefield Design (www.battlefield-design.co.uk)
Printed by Short Run Press, Exeter, Devon

Text from the 1901 edition edited by Mrs S.C.I. Wood and published by Simpkin, Marshall,
Hamilton, Kent, & Co., London. Introduction, notes, and commentary © Andrew Bamford 2017.
Illustrations © as individually credited
Maps © David Beckford 2017

Cover: The 12th Light Dragoons at Waterloo (Watercolour by William Barnes-Wollen, ©
9th/12th Royal Lancers Regimental Museum, Derby)

ISBN 978-1-911512-32-5

British Library Cataloguing-in-Publication Data.
A catalogue record for this book is available from the British Library.

For details of other military history titles published by Helion & Company Limited, contact
the above address, or visit our website: http://www.helion.co.uk

We always welcome receiving book proposals from prospective authors.

Contents

List of Illustrations

List of Maps

New Introduction

Some years ago, seeking a British cavalry regiment of the Napoleonic era to form the basis of a case-study, I set upon the 12th Light Dragoons. The primary reason for that choice was the existence of a vast amount of useful official correspondence in the archives of the regimental museum, but in the process of putting together my book on the regiment I discovered that there were also several excellent primary accounts of service in the Napoleonic Wars left by officers who had served in the 12th. One of those officers was John Vandeleur, whose letters – originally privately published – have since reissued, with notes and commentary by myself, under the title *With Wellington's Outposts*. Another such officer, and the only other to produce a book-length account, was William Hay.

In many respects, Hay and Vandeleur have a lot in common. Both were graduates of the Royal Military College at Marlow – in itself, a rare thing in an age when few British officers had the benefit of a formal military education – and both were initially commissioned into light infantry regiments before transferring to light cavalry. Both, too, had family connections – rather more illustrious ones in Hay's case than Vandeleur's – that took them from regimental duty to spend time on the personal staffs of senior officers. Both officers, therefore, were well placed to write interesting and informative accounts of their service, but there the similarity ends. Whereas Vandeleur's letters were written at the time, Hay composed his account over a quarter-century after the events in question. This gives them a very different perspective. Unpleasant ordeals recorded by Vandeleur had often faded into amusing anecdotes by the time Hay came to record them, and Hay's account has the benefit of hindsight and reflection but at the cost of the immediacy that comes from Vandeleur.

Where the strengths of Hay's account come out is his frankness. Although neither officer was writing with a view to publication – Vandeleur to his parents and Hay for the amusement of his daughter – Hay is surprisingly honest about some of the more disreputable aspects of service and the advantage that was sometimes taken of the Spanish and Portuguese people, reporting liberties taken, and pranks played, that Vandeleur obviously though better of reporting to his family. At the same time, however, Hay does have something of the character of a British Marbot about him, always the hero of his own epic be that in terms of military exploits or bets won against fellow-officers. On those occasions when his desire to tell a good story call the veracity of his account into question, which is particularly apparent in his treatment of the events of the Hundred Days, I have added a footnote to that effect.

Otherwise, footnotes have been used to identify people and places, to add additional supporting information to place Hay's narrative in context, and, on occasion, to highlight some of the occasions when he and Vandeleur are quite clearly describing the same events or when their accounts otherwise compliment one and other. The basic text remains as far as possible as per the 1901 first edition which was introduced and edited by Hay's daughter; on the few occasions where it has been easier to make a correction or clarification in the main body of the text rather than in a footnote, square brackets have been used to indicate where this has been done. However, I have taken the liberty of breaking the account into more manageable chapters than was the case for the original edition, in which the bulk of the text covering Hay's wartime experiences was presented as a single block, followed by two short sections respectively covering his post-war exploits in Canada, where he served on the staff of Lord Dalhousie during the latter's tenure as Governor General of British North America, and his final years of home service prior to retirement.

Rather than repeat the same citations over again, it should be noted that, unless otherwise cited, all biographical information about persons mentioned in the text is taken from Robert Burnham (ed.), "Lionel S. Challis' 'Peninsula Roll Call'", at http://www.napoleon-series.org/research/biographies/GreatBritain/Challis/c_ChallisIntro.html and Charles Dalton, *The Waterloo Roll Call* (London: Eyre and Spottiwoode, 1904), supplemented for Chapter IV with material from the *Dictionary of Canadian Biography*.

The original 1901 edition of Hay's memoir was edited by his daughter, Mrs Sarah Wood, who also provided it with a short introduction the bulk of which served to dedicate the work to Field Marshal Lord Roberts, hero of then-ongoing Second Boer War. It is unclear to what extent the original narrative was cut in Mrs Wood's editing process; however, since the story that is presented is complete in its essentials, it can be safely assumed that her editorial touch was a light one, perhaps only restricted to the attempt to disguise the names of individuals of whom her father had expressed a low opinion. For completeness, Mrs Wood's original 1901 introduction is reproduced below:

> In my preface to the manuscript of my father's "Reminiscences and Anecdotes," which I lent to private friends and relatives for perusal, I mentioned they were written, at my earnest request, during the few leisure hours he had in the midst of a busy life, as Commissioner of Police of the Metropolis, from 1840 to 1855.
>
> He began by relating a few particulars of our family, which, with the account following of his military life, are given in his own words.
>
> The extraordinary facility with which over a quarter of a million men and scores of thousands of horses and mules have been recently

transported safely thousands of miles in an incredibly short space of time, and the admirable commissariat and other arrangements of the present war in South Africa, induce me to think that the record of his campaigning and fighting experiences, during the Peninsular War and Waterloo, as a subaltern in both infantry and cavalry, under the Duke of Wellington, will be read with much interest by a far wider circle, if only as a comparison in many ways.

May the anecdotes give as much pleasure to others as they did to me, when I listened to them as a girl!

I have to express my sincere gratitude to Field Marshal Earl Roberts for the trouble taken in procuring for me a correct representation of the regimental colours of the old 52nd Light Infantry, now the 1st Oxfordshire Light Infantry – that of the 12th Light Dragoons, it appears, is unattainable – and also for his usual and universally known good-heartedness in "gladly consenting" to my dedicating these pages to him, which I feel to be one of the greatest honours that could be paid to the memory of my father.

I have to thank A. Sidney Morton, the son of a very dear old friend now passed away, for assisting me in preparing the work for publication.

S. C. I. WOOD.
LITTLETHORPE HOUSE,
RIPON

There is, perhaps, little that Hay's recollections can add to our understanding of the course of the great events in which he took part. His memory for detail cannot always be relied upon – something which I have noted on those occasions where it leads him into an obvious inaccuracy – and his accounts of most of the major battles in which he took part are sketchy: Fuentes de Oñoro, in which his regiment was heavily engaged, is dismissed in a single sentence. Waterloo, however, seems to have made an impression even on an officer who had by this point served four years in the Peninsula and taken part in several major battles, and his account serves to give a vivid impression of the horror and confusion of that cramped and bloody field. That aside, though, the real value in Hay's narrative is the personal view that it gives into the mind-set of a young officer of the era. As Hay gets into one of his anecdotes, one can feel the years fall away and the young subaltern – sometimes brash, occasionally even arrogant, and never entirely serious – comes back to the fore. More than anything it is this vivid impression of the author as a young man that represents the true and lasting value of this text.

Andrew Bamford, March 2017

1

Beginnings, Marlow, and the 52nd

Our family is descended from John, first Marquis of Tweedale; your great-great-grandfather being Lord Alexander, his third son. He married Katherine Kerr, an heiress, who had property in Berwickshire and East Lowthian. His estates were Lawfield, Springfield, Mereside, East Barnes, and Spott, the residence of the family. His brothers were the Marquis of Tweeddale, Lord William Hay of Newton, and Lord David Hay of Belton. His only sister married Robert, [2nd] Duke of Roxburgh. Lord Alexander had three sons, Robert, John, and William, and one daughter, who married Sir Robert Anstruther. His two eldest sons dying, he was succeeded by your great-grandfather, William, who married the daughter of Sir Robert Sinclair of Stevenson. One of her brothers took the name of Lockhart, of Castlehill, Lanarkshire.

William Hay had three sons and five daughters. John, died young; William, who entered the 83rd Regiment, also died young;[1] and your grandfather, Robert, who was also a soldier in the same regiment, succeeded to the property. He married Catherine, daughter of Ralph Babington, Esq., of Greenfort, Co. Donegal, and had thirteen children, of whom I, William, am the eldest.

After my birth, which took place at the family residence, Spott House, near Dunbar, on October 14, 1792, my father and mother (having left me in the care of my grandmother living at Beanston) removed to Ireland where his regiment was quartered.

Some time after the birth of my eldest sister my father left the Army, and came home to live.[2] Finding his property a good deal encumbered, he sold Lawfield,

---

1   Captain William Hay of the 83rd (County of Dublin) Regiment, died 14 November 1795, apparently of disease, whilst the regiment was serving in the West Indies. See Bray, William Edward, et al, *Memoirs and Services of the Eighty-Third Regiment, County of Dublin, From 1793 to 1907* (London: Hugh Rees, 1908), p.15

2   The London Gazette (No. 13708, p.987) records that Captain William Godley was promoted on 22 August 1794 into the majority left vacant by Robert Hay's resignation from the 83rd. William Hay's sister, Catherine, was born on 9 February of the same year, placing the family's return to Spott between those two dates.

which cleared him; and I began my infant life as heir to a large and, in those days, valuable property. Events proved, however, there is nothing certain but death.

Till the age of eight I was educated by my grandmother and the village clergyman. In 1800 I was sent to what had the reputation of being a good country-school at Musselburgh. The wife of the master, Taylor, was kind and careful of the boys; but Mr. Taylor himself was a careless, self-indulgent man. This reaching the ears of my father, I was removed, and for a few months remained at home under a private tutor, who was in charge of my younger brothers. But my father's house being usually full of guests, principally military men, the gaiety of the surroundings drove all idea of study out of my head, and it was found necessary to again send me to school, at Edinburgh, where for a time I remained, attending the different classes held by the best masters of the day.

My father having decided to prepare me for the Army, it was arranged for me to be sent to the Royal Military College, Marlow. Accordingly, application was made to Sir Henry Calvert, an old brother officer and intimate friend of my father, at that time adjutant-general, who at once undertook not only to have me admitted to the Royal Military College, but, as soon as by study I became eligible, to recommend me to the Duke of York for a commission.[3]

In 1807 I was started from Spott under the care of our old butler and with a young lad named Spiers as a companion, who, like myself, was about to join the college.[4]

In those days steamboats and railways were unknown, we therefore posted the whole journey, being allowed to spend two days in London, as we passed through, to see the sights.

It was in the time of the autumn examinations we reached Great Marlow, and every inn in the small town full, and beds not to be had; we managed to pass the night, but the next day was a more serious affair. Everything was new to me, a raw Scotch boy! I felt truly lost! The examination began; and the Latin I got through well enough, but when arithmetic was put before me I became bewildered and lost my head, consequently was turned back, with many more unfortunates.

I then went to the house of the Rev. Knowles for further preparation; and in a month's time was admitted to the Royal Military College, and appointed to C

3   Established in 1802 under the aegis of then-colonel, later Major General, John Gaspard Le Marchant, the Junior Department of the Royal Military College was situated at Marlow and intended to prepare young men for service as officers in regiments either of the British Army or that of the Honourable East India Company. This was distinct from the Senior Department at High Wycombe, which trained serving officers in staff duties.

4   Hay's companion was Alexander J. Spiers, or Spears, who was commissioned without purchase into the 39th Foot on 29 June 1809 and who served with that regiment in the Peninsula and North America, being promoted to a lieutenancy on 25 October 1810. He was severely wounded at Vitoria, for which action he received a Silver Medal.

'Great Marlow. The Royal Military College': hand-coloured engraving, London, Parker.
(Anne SK Brown Collection)

Company, commanded by Captain Erskine (a natural son of the Earl of Buchan!) – my number was C. 29.[5]

The rules of the college were strictly according to military code and regulations, with certain classes, and no cadet was eligible for a commission until he attained the upper fourth in arithmetic, French, landscape and military drawing, etc. There were, however, no particular punishments for idleness, so if your conduct was, in other respects good, the professor gave himself little concern as to your application.

The effect of such leniency was to make me ten times more idle, though I took care not to commit myself as far as conduct went. Hence, every summer, when I went home, brought my poor, kind father the same mortifying report, viz. – 'Conduct good, progress not equal to the time employed.'

---

5   Hay's company commander was Captain Sir David Erskine, whose knighthood was bestowed for his care of the Fitzclarence brothers, natural sons of HRH the Duke of Clarence, when they were gentleman cadets at Marlow. Erskine would later come into a sizeable inheritance from his natural father, the 11th Earl, upon the latter's death in 1829 and was a founder member of the Scottish Military and Naval Academy. See obituary in the *Gentleman's Magazine*, Vol.VIII (New Series) Jul-Dec1838, p.652.

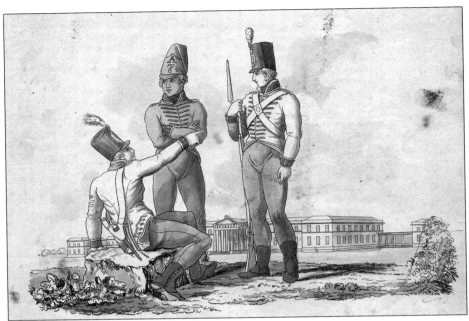

'Cadets at the Royal Military College of Sandhurst Junior Department': original drawing from 'C. H. Smith. Costume of the British Army'. (Anne S.K. Brown Military Collection)

I delighted in my military duties, and often volunteered to take guard for others. It was while doing this one morning, I heard a speech which entirely cured my idleness.

Colonel Butler, my chief, used to drill the cadets on parade every morning, at eleven o'clock-the guard turning out to present arms, when he appeared. He then made an inspection of the ranks; being very short-sighted, if he wished to recognise any particular cadet, he had to look very closely. I happened that morning to be right-hand front rank, he therefore began with me; he stopped, looked hard in my face, looked again, repeated my name, and then said: 'Fine young man! What a pity you don't pay more attention to your studies! I fear you will get into a scrape!'[6]

My heart almost sprang into my mouth, for I was shocked and mortified, but I took a decided resolution, and, without saying anything to my comrades, who

6   Lieutenant Colonel James Butler, Royal Artillery, commandant of the Junior School. Butler subsequently became Lieutenant-Governor of the Royal Military College in succession to its founder, Le Marchant, with whom he had previously clashed. Described as bulky, choleric, and extremely short-sighted, with a penchant for strict discipline. See Thoumine, R.H., *Scientific Soldier. A Life of General Le Marchant 1766-1812* (Oxford: Oxford University Press, 1968), pp.84-92.

were all anxious to hear what the commandant had said, I went to study that afternoon and so worked, that in four and a half months I had passed every examination, and reached fourth form! On receiving the, at length, satisfactory report, my father claimed Sir H. Calvert's promise, and asked for an ensigncy.

In answer, a letter came from the adjutant-general saying he had recommended me to His Royal Highness for a commission in the 52nd Light Infantry, it having been the express wish of the famous Sir John Moore, who, as an old and intimate friend of both my father and Sir H. Calvert, had desired that I should begin my military life in his own regiment and under his own protection. This latter, alas! I could not do, as Sir John had been killed the year before. But, Sir H. Calvert, carrying out his wish, I found myself gazetted to the distinguished and gallant corps; and, to my no small satisfaction, with two ensigns under me whose names were in the same gazette.[7]

At the youthful age of sixteen I joined my regiment, the rules of which at that time were most strict and perfect for young officers, having been drawn up by Sir John Moore himself. The sum he stipulated as yearly allowance in addition to pay was not to exceed £100; but £80 he considered sufficient to enable an officer to live as a gentleman, without getting into debt. My father allowed me the larger sum.

When I joined the 2nd battalion of the 52nd it was quartered at Chatham barracks, under Sir J. Ross.[8]

My reception was kind and friendly, and I found among the young officers several who had been my companions at Marlow. Placed in the company of Captain, afterwards Sir William, Chambers [sic], I, with the other youngsters, was handed over to the Adjutant, Lieutenant Shaw, for drill, it being the rule of the regiment that all young officers must be drilled for six months in the ranks with the men before being allowed to do duty as an officer.[9] These drills consisted of

7   Hay was commissioned ensign without purchase, with seniority dated to 30 January 1810. The two officers gazetted as his juniors were ensigns Robert Smith (31 January) and David Walker (1 February). Both these officers, however, took some time joining the regiment, which meant that Hay was still the most junior subaltern actually present for duty when he joined the 2/52nd. Such was the turnover of officers, however, that after six months Hay was the most senior of the battalion's ensigns. It is not clear exactly when Hay joined his battalion: the Monthly Return of 25 February 1810 lists him as not yet joined, but he was present for duty a month later. See The National Archives (hereafter, TNA), WO17/167.

8   Lt. Colonel Sir John Ross, who had commanded the 2/52nd during the Coruna campaign and who would command the 1/52nd in the Peninsula from November 1810 until July 1811. Subsequently served in Ceylon and Ireland and eventually rose to the rank of lieutenant general.

9   Either Hay's memory or the accuracy of his original editor is at fault here: the officer in question was Captain William Chalmers, not Chambers. First commissioned in 1803, he served with the 2/52nd on Sicily, in the Peninsula 1808-1809, and at Walcheren, subsequently with 1/52nd in the Peninsula 1811-1815 but primarily as a brigade major rather than on regimental duty. After serving with his regiment at Waterloo, he went on to become a lieutenant general and, as Hay rightly says, a knight. The adjutant of the 2/52nd was Lieutenant Abraham Shaw, later a captain in the 2nd West India Regiment.

'An officer and private of the 52nd Ryl. Lt. Infantry': original drawing from
'C. H. Smith. Costume of the British Army'. (Anne S.K. Brown Military Collection)

five hours each day, besides morning and evening parades, and we were kept well occupied with our military duties.

The 2nd battalion of the 52nd had a few months before arrived from the disastrous campaign of Walcheren and, in consequence of the dreadful fever caught there, the hospitals were full and the ranks thin of men, five, six, and sometimes ten a day dying. At first I was shocked to see so many funerals, but I was soon to find that a soldier quickly becomes reconciled to seeing death in all shapes.

Between military duties by day, and amusing ourselves as boys, by racing against each other in the evening, our time passed quickly. Chatham was a delightful quarter, there being a large garrison of three battalions of Militia, Artillery, and Marines besides our own. This gave a constant change of society. I was soon destined to see my first campaign, and that, of all places, in London.

At that period, as history tells us, opinions on the 'liberty of the subject', as it was called by the Liberal party, ran high; and amongst the number of advocates for popular excitement was the, late Sir Francis Burdett, member for Westminster. He had become troublesome and committed himself to such an extent that Government considered it necessary to send him to the Tower; and a disturbance was in consequence apprehended, and all the military within several days' march were ordered to, and to be quartered in, London.[10]

When standing on our usual morning garrison parade for guard-mounting the London post came in, and by it the route was received for the 52nd to march at once for the expected scene of action. Parade was dismissed and orders issued to assemble in an hour in marching order, and that afternoon we started on our way to Dartford. The next day we arrived at Trotter's warehouse, Dean Street, Soho (later the well-known Soho Bazaar), which was pointed out as the post to be occupied by our corps. A pallet of straw and one blanket were given to each officer and soldier, and in the long lofts of the warehouse we were domiciled, pickets posted, and every precaution taken to meet and repel any outbreak which might occur. The men were strictly confined to quarters, the officers were allowed a range of about two hundred yards down Dean Street and to a small coffee house known by the name of Morley's which remains much the same at the present day, and at which I often look, when passing that neighbourhood, with a sad recollection of what were then such happy days, for I was a soldier at heart and was delighted with the novelty and change, caring nothing for the discomforts.

We remained about three weeks in London, when the events, for which we had been sent there, having passed off quietly, we were ordered to return to Chatham. This we were to do by going down the river as far as Gravesend in large, flat-bottomed boats, to convey troops (steamboats being unknown) carrying about one hundred men each. By some accident the great unwieldy concern, in which Captain Chambers' [sic] company was embarked, ran aground and could not be got off. We disembarked, and marched by the dusty road, making a day's work of some twenty-two miles before reaching Gravesend. Next morning we proceeded to our old quarters at Chatham, where we found our more fortunate companions ready to receive us, and drills and field-days proceeded as before.

---

10 A political radical of long standing – he had, amongst other things, opposed war with France, opposed the suspension of the Habeus Corpus Act, supported fellow-radical Horne Tooke when it was proposed to prevent him taking a seat at Westminster, and taken part in the campaign to have the Duke of York removed as Commander-in-Chief of the Army as a result of the Mary Anne Clarke scandal – Burdett had been arrested on a charge of libelling the House of Commons after allowing the publication in the *Weekly Register* a speech that he had made, questioning the legality of the House having yet another radical, John Gale Jones, committed to prison.

In May of that year we received orders for the battalion to move to Ashford, also in Kent.[11] The weather was hot and the roads dusty. Our first day's march was to Maidstone, the second to Ashford over a very hilly road. Our officers, who could afford to keep horses, by the kind indulgence of Colonel Ross, were allowed to ride after leaving the town in which we were billeted, dismounting before arriving at our next quarters. Among those who benefited in this way was a most gentlemanly and good fellow, Lieutenant Kerr. On our arrival at Ashford, when the men were dismissed, we officers, covered with heat and dust – at least those who, like myself, had walked the whole march – were in the messroom getting what refreshment we could; my friend Kerr came in and began in a good-humoured way to quiz me for being knocked up. I told him he never was more mistaken, and notwithstanding I had walked the whole march and he had not, I was ready to start against him and go back! This retort amused our mutual friends who were by, and I was immediately backed by many to beat Kerr. What I had offered in joke I could not retreat from, as my honour was at stake. I did not bet a farthing myself, but, as many of my companions had, I was willing to do my best for them. Kerr had the reputation of being a rich man.[12]

In ten minutes umpires were named, and we were started to walk back the road we had just travelled, attended by our backers and friends. Off we went, and for the first eight or nine miles I and my adversary kept pretty even; but after that, though the younger and slighter of the two, and feeling myself ready to expire from the heat, I got a start, and on I went and was soon out of sight of my friend Kerr, to the no small satisfaction of my backers. After proceeding a few miles further, our companions, thinking we had both done enough in one day, called a truce; and Kerr acknowledged himself well beaten, making an offer to pay half his bets. Having no stake myself I had no voice, but all agreed to the arrangement which I was by no means sorry for. We returned to a country inn near, and had a merry dinner, and drove back to our barracks in postchaises.

After very few months' experience as a soldier, I began to take my work more easily and to look about for amusements, my great friend and companion being Lieutenant Hamilton, a nephew of the late Sir John Moore;[13] he, like myself, was devoted to every kind of field sport, to indulge in which taste we kept dogs and

11   The 2/52nd was in London at the time of the 25 April 1810 Monthly Return, but was again listed at Chatham in that for May. The station is given as Ashford for the first time in the return of 25 June. If Hay is correct that the battalion marched for Ashford in May, then it must have been during the last week of that month.

12   The identity of this officer is a mystery; no-one of that surname served with the 52nd at this time. Whether this is another mistake, as with Chambers/Chalmers, or Hay was deliberately concealing the identity of this officer, is not clear.

13   Lt. Douglas John Hamilton, who served several stints in the Peninsula with both battalions of the 52nd before being promoted to a captaincy in the 85th in January 1813. Subsequently served with that regiment in North America and was killed in action at Bladensburg.

ferrets, and with them hunted rats in old barns, and rabbits in hedgerows. On one of these excursions we were surprised and made prisoners by the gamekeeper of Lord Thanet who had been watching us.

He read the Game Act, and seized our stock-in-trade – nets, ferrets, etc.; but after the first brush and angry words had passed, a conciliatory invitation was given to our friend in the green jacket to come and see us at Mrs., or, rather, mother Myers', who kept a fruit shop in Ashford, and where we used to assemble after morning drill to eat strawberries-and-cream.

Our invitation, after the judicious tip of half-a-crown, was accepted; and next morning our guest was punctual at ten o'clock to his appointment, when, after the admiration of various glasses of Mrs. Myers' strong brandy-and-water, he not only restored our nets and ferrets, but gave us a hint that whenever we wished for a day's, or, rather, night's sport we should meet him in a certain wood he named. The result of this invitation was, we were both absent from drill; and, as a consequence a report made to the commanding officer.

Next morning the colonel's servant called betimes, bringing me an invitation to breakfast with his master. After drill Colonel Ross and my kind friend, then Major Gibbs (afterwards Lieutenant-General and Lieutenant-Governor of Jersey), were ready to receive Hamilton and myself.[14] An excellent breakfast, during which we were treated with the greatest kindness and attention, being despatched, the colonel told us the major had something to communicate. He then left us with that kindest and best of men in command, and from him we received an admonition as to our misconduct of poaching, absence from drill, etc., etc., an admonition which went far deeper than a much more severe censure would have done.

The weather, it being now July, was very hot, and our military duties and light infantry movements and skirmishing all over the country, were severe. Returning from one of these, much heated, I imprudently drank some cold water and sat in a draught, the result being a severe chill and scarlet fever.

I believe my illness was considerably increased owing to intelligence received that evening by the commanding officer, that all officers of the 1st battalion, then in Portugal, were to proceed forthwith to join the battalion. My horror and distress are not to be described when told by the doctor my moving, for at least some weeks, was quite out of the question. However, Colonel Ross gave me his word that, whenever I was reported able to undertake the journey to Portsmouth, I should be allowed to follow my more fortunate comrades, who had started two days after for the Peninsula.

---

14   Major Edward Gibbs. Having already served on Sicily and in the Coruna campaign, he returned to the Peninsula in March 1811 and served with the 1/52nd until invalided home after losing an eye at Badajoz by which time he was a brevet lieutenant colonel and acting as a brigade commander in the Light Division. Subsequently served again in the Peninsula May-August 1813, then commanded 2/52nd in the Low Countries 1813-1814.

Next week brought an order for our battalion to change quarters to Shorncliffe barracks.[15] I had to remain behind for a few days till the fever had abated; but youth and a good constitution shook off indisposition, and in August I was able to claim Colonel Ross's promise, and with the assistant-surgeon, Dr. Walker, took my departure for London and Portsmouth, as our first step towards joining our regiment in Portugal. On writing to tell my father of my destination, I received a most affectionate letter of advice from my mother, accompanied by the unsolicited gift of £50.[16]

I proceeded to London by coach, and put up at the Golden Cross, Charing Cross, then a horrid, dirty hole, and soon discovered that every advantage was taken of the unfortunate officers about to join their regiments abroad. Money had of course to be changed for the currency of the country; I remember I had, in exchanging my country note for Bank of England ones, to pay 2s. in the £, and two or three more again in exchanging these for Portugal doubloons.

On arriving at Portsmouth, I found no orders had been given for the fleet sailing, but a convoy was expected to get under weigh soon. On calling on the commandant I received an order for a passage on a small brig, leaving with stores for Lisbon, called the *Elizabeth*, commanded by Captain Banks; to her I repaired, and, little as I cared for personal pleasures and comforts in general, I must confess I was somewhat shocked at what was to be my lodging for the next few weeks. The small, close cabin, to say nothing of the strong smell of bilge-water coming from the confined hold of that miserable little transport, were anything but luxurious.

On my return to shore I went in one of the ship's boat's, to save the expense of a waterman's boat – hundreds of which were plying for hire amongst the fleet of ships assembled at Spithead. There was a stiff wind blowing, and the sea ran high; the boat in which I had taken my passage was only manned by two ship's boys, who took a delight in trying to frighten me – a landsman as they thought – by keeping her broadside on to the seas, drenching us to the skin. In the midst of their pranks – which I had sufficient command over myself to pretend not to notice – we got near the shore and among the breakers, one large wave lifting us high and dry on the shore, up which I had to scramble quickly enough to escape being carried out to sea by the returning wave; and in my drenched clothing found my way to my rooms at the well-known Blue Posts inn.

Daily I called on the agent for transports, but he gave little hope of a speedy departure. Troops kept arriving, and transports collecting; but it was not till October that the 'Blue Peters' were hoist, and signal guns fired to call us aboard.

---

15   The 2/52nd is first recorded as being at Shorncliffe in the Monthly Return of 25 August 1810, by which time Hay is listed as present but belonging to the regiment's first battalion.

16   Assistant-Surgeon Thomas Walker, a veteran of substantial prior service in the Peninsula, who was returning to the 1/52nd after a very short spell in Britain. He was promoted to surgeon in the 52nd in 1812 and to Physician the following year. In that Hay is not listed as present in the Monthly Return of 25 September, he and Walker had evidently departed before then.

I bade adieu without regret to the scene of my weary waiting, and joined five other officers, also about to join their several regiments at Lisbon. I did not admire the conduct of my companions sufficiently for them to make a favourable impression on my mind. One, a good-natured, red-faced captain of the 45th, used to amuse me – or himself – by playing draughts with me in the evening, and succeeded in depriving me of fifty dollars – a no small sum for an ensign to lose![17] We had a most stormy and rough passage, entering the Tagus after a thirty days' voyage.

On my arrival at Lisbon I found my companions, who had started a long time before me, had encountered so many delays – more even than I had done – that they were only then about to start to join the Army. A few days were allowed for us newcomers to provide ourselves with mules, etc., and we were then all to proceed together towards our different destinations. I supplied myself with a small, but good mule, for which I paid £12 10s.

The animal's business was to carry myself and kit, which consisted of only what could be stowed away in a very small pair of saddle-bags, little thinking how long it would be ere I had a chance to replenish my wardrobe! But in those days I concerned myself little as to provision for the morrow. I was contented, happy, and quite ready to go through the rough work of a soldier's life, so soon to begin in earnest.

After sundry adventures, too trifling to notice, we arrived, and reported ourselves at the headquarters of the 52nd Light Infantry, two evenings after the battle of Busaco.[18]

The Light Division, in which the 52nd was a leading regiment, was at the time in the rear of the whole army, covering the retreat – several of the officers had been killed and wounded in the late engagements; amongst the latter was my father's old friend, Colonel Berkeley, who, notwithstanding his own misfortune, had not forgotten me – a young lad, soon to come under his protection. He had, before his removal to the rear, left particular instructions with another kind friend, Captain Mayne, senior captain of regiment, to see that I was placed in the company of an officer who would look after a youngster. I was attached to the company of Captain

---

17   This officer was Captain John O'Flaherty, on his way to join the 1/45th in the Peninsula where he would serve for the rest of the war. See Brown, Steve, *Wellington's Redjackets: The 45th (Nottinghamshire) Regiment on Campaign in South America and the Peninsula, 1805-1814* (Barnsley: Frontline, 2015).

18   This assertion does not fit with the dates established elsewhere in the narrative, since Busaco was fought on 27 September and Hay reports being still at Portsmouth into October. The first Monthly Return for the 1/52nd in which Hay appears as present with the battalion is that for 25 November 1810, on which date it is listed as being stationed at 'Valle', which would seem to be Vale de Santarém situated just west of the town of Santarém. This corresponds with the rest of Hay's narrative and would suggest that he in fact joined his new battalion after Wellington's withdrawal into the Lines of Torres Vedras, subsequently advancing with it in mid-November when the French fell back on Santarém and the Light Division was part of the force pushed up towards that place to keep them under observation.

Douglas, a most worthy, excellent man, and a brave soldier. (Poor Colonel Berkeley died of his wounds after his arrival in England.)[19]

I had certainly heard much of soldiering, campaigning, fighting, etc., but I little dreamed what it really was. The weather was wet and cold, and the roads in the most dreadful state, and I shall never forget the shock to my nervous system on seeing the careless way the bodies of dead men were trodden on as we passed them lying in the muddy roads! But I soon became accustomed to such sights. On our march we were for several days pressed by the advance guards of the French, and when we encamped for the night, our pickets and theirs were within a few paces of each other.

(I do not intend to attempt a history of the Peninsular War, but merely to give a sketch of my own proceedings with the army; therefore shall only observe here, that, after a few more days' retreat, the Light Division were brought up to a small but beautiful town at the bottom of one of the hills, which compose the base of the heights of Torres Vedras – well known by the famous lines constructed by the Duke of Wellington – not only as a place of safe retreat for our army, but as a barrier and protection for Lisbon against the advancing enemy, under General [sic – Marshal] Massena.)

On taking up our quarters the soldiers were left in the streets instead of being put up in the houses of the town. My astonishment was great to see the camp-fires lighted up by the help of costly furniture, the parties from each company sent to find fuel to cook the rations and dry the clothing, arms, etc., returning bearing chairs, tables, and all kinds of valuable articles which were broken up and used as if they were so much rotten wood.

Here we remained in advance of the Army, enduring great privations and hard-ships, for some five or six weeks, when, one morning, we found the enemy had disappeared from our front. On we went after them, and for some days ploughed our way through ponds of mud – for they did not deserve the name of roads – continuing to advance as long as the French army retreated, which was for about five days; we halted on the banks of a small river, the enemy occupying the heights of Santarem; here the Light Division went into what are called cantonments. This one being a sort of large farmyard surrounded by a low wall. A few houses which had been cleared of all furniture – even doors and windows taken from their frames – were allotted to the officers, the men being in a field in front. My bed was half an old window-shutter, but on which I enjoyed most sound sleep, though my

---

19 There are some misspellings here. 'Berkeley' was Lt. Colonel Robert Barclay, who was severely wounded at Busaco whilst commanding the brigade of which the 1/52nd was a part, and who died of his wounds on 3 May 1811. 'Mayne' was Captain William Mein, who served on with the battalion until the end of 1813 and who ended the war a major and a brevet lieutenant colonel. The only officer in this trio whose surname has been given correctly is Captain John Graham Douglas, Hay's company commander, who had been with the battalion throughout its Peninsular service and who would remain with it until his death on 24 December 1813 in consequence of wounds received at the Nivelle two weeks previously.

only covering was a camlet boat-cloak; my clothes were never off my back, or my shoes off my feet any night during that winter.

There was a long bridge and causeway over the river leading to Santarem, at one end of which our pickets were posted; at the other, the French had theirs; sentinels being about fifty yards apart in the middle of the bridge. Our quarters, in the houses I spoke of, were about two miles from this bridge and of course all hands on the outposts had to be pretty much on the alert. The regimental bugles sounded to turn out every morning an hour before daybreak, and we stood under arms until an hour after sunrise. After the duty was over we amused ourselves riding, walking, or in the best way we could. It was while we were here an event happened which I did not at all relish; it was the first actual bloodshed I had witnessed. Attached to the Light Division was a regiment of foreigners – French, Germans, and others, some of whom had volunteered their services to us hoping that the chances of war would enable them to get back to their own country.

One night, after we had retired to rest, we were called up by the alarm sounding 'To Arms'; several shots were fired toward the front. It turned out, however, to be fourteen of those unfortunate men making an attempt to desert to the enemy. Some were shot by the picket, and five were taken prisoners. These were tried by court-martial, and condemned to be shot. The division was drawn up for the purpose, and the sentence carried into execution on four of them; the fifth, a mere child, was pardoned, after having had his eyes bandaged, etc. The whole spectacle I did not forget for some time.[20]

Early in March, 1811, the French broke up their position and we pushed on after them. I was getting used to horrid sights, but was terribly shocked at seeing the number of dead and dying, as we marched past, lying in the roadside. Our own men knocked up, and those of the enemy – poor fellows – alike unable to go further. My own kit, which, as I told you was a very limited one, was in a sad plight! My stockings were worn out and I replaced them by strips of blanket laid in my shoes, which, too, were well-worn by constant marching.

We were moving all day and arrived, very tired with little and frequently nothing to eat, on some hillside where the French had taken up their position for the night. An hour before daybreak we were at it again, till at last we brought them

20 On 12 November 1810, nine companies of the Brunswick-Oels Light Infantry were transferred from the Fourth Division to the Light Division but had been returned to the Fourth Division before 1 February 1811, presumably to keep them away from the outposts and the temptations of desertion: the battalion ultimately found a home in the Seventh Division with which it served for the remainder of the war. See C.T. Atkinson's appendix to Oman, Sir Charles, *Wellington's Army 1809-1814* (London: Edward Arnold, 1913), pp.349, 355. During this time, the Brunswick-Oels Light Infantry lost 24 deserters in the month to 25 November 1810, 2 in the month to 25 December 1810, and 36 in the month to 25 January 1811, for a total of 62 (a little under nine per cent of the battalion's initial rank and file strength), although it is likely that at least some of these came from the three detached jäger companies serving with the Fourth and Fifth Divisions. See Monthly Returns for the Peninsular Army, TNA, WO17/2465, /2467.

to a standstill at a place called Pombal; here the first sharp fight I had seen took place, engaging us all day.

This commenced a series of engagements – first, Pombal; second, Redinha; third, Condacia; fourth, Fez de Aronce.[21] At the latter place a sight astonished me: about five hundred donkeys were sitting and lying in the muddy road all hamstrung by their brutal masters, the French, rather than allow them to fall into our hands.

We now resumed our march, and did not come up with the French till we arrived at the banks of the River Coa. There we had a very hard fight.[22] From that battle we followed the enemy to the frontiers of Spain. There we had quarters in a neat, clean, Spanish village named Gallegos, the French being two miles off in our front. I was now accustomed to this kind of life, the activity and excitement suiting me exactly.[23]

At Gallegos I was enabled to take off my clothes and get into bed for the first time for seven months. Here our time was passed between duties and riding about to see the country (and, as this is not to be a history of the movements of the Army, but an account of my personal experiences, I will tell you of the small adventure I met with here). We had one day some sharp fighting, and many men and horses were killed on both sides. The day after, when all was quiet, I, with one or two other officers, rode out to look at the ground we had fought over. On the face of the hill, where were many corpses, we found some hundreds of large, white-headed eagles hard at work feeding on them. We at once drew swords and prepared to charge them; as the birds were so gorged it was difficult for them to get on the wing. The little horse on which I was mounted was very quick, and in a few moments carried me into the midst of the group of monster birds, at the head of one of which I made a cut, but he struck my little nag with his wing which caused him to rear and fall back on me. No bones were broken, but I was stiff and hurt for some days and grievously disappointed at my bird having got off without his share of hurt.

Some weeks after this the battle of Fuentes d'Onore took place, in which the Light Division were hotly engaged. Having, however, as usual, beaten the French, we returned to our old quarters in the frontier villages. Here the French again attacked our outposts and we retired before them.[24]

---

21   These were the actions at Pombal, 11 March 1811; Redinha, 12 March; Casal Novo, 14 March (the village of Condeixa, by which Hay and also some French accounts name this action, was some way from the actual scene of the fighting); Foz do Arouce, 15 March. See Smith, Digby, *The Greenhill Napoleonic Wars Data Book* (London: Greenhill, 1998), pp.355-256.

22   The Battle of Sabugal, 3 April 1811. See Smith, *Data Book*, pp.357-358; Oman, Sir Charles, *A History of the Peninsular War* (Oxford: Oxford University Press, 1902-1930), Vol. IV, pp.189-198. It would seem likely that the anecdote related in the next paragraph relates to the aftermath of this action, as the Light Division was not seriously engaged again before Fuentes de Oñoro.

23   Gallegos de Argañán, 12 miles west of Ciudad Rodrigo.

24   The Battle of Fuentes de Oñoro was fought 3-5 May 1811 and saw Massena's Armée du Portugal defeated and prevented from relieving the French garrison of Almeida. It is to be regretted that Hay did

'Battle of Fuentes D'Onor, taken from the right of the position occupied by the 1st, 3rd and 7th Divisions on the 5th May, 1811': Aquatint by Chares Turner after Thomas St Clair.
(Anne S.K. Brown Military Collection)

The weather at this time (the month of July) was awfully hot, and many of the men fell down dead, struck by the sun. After a march of some twelve or fifteen days we arrived near Badajoz, where we encamped on an open plain for at least six weeks, after which we began our return march to the north of Portugal.[25]

After some days' progress I was directed, as first 'sub' for duty, to remain behind with a few men to take charge of a store of ammunition until I had an opportunity to give it over to some other regiment following our line of march. The place where I halted was called Neeza – a small, dirty town – the inhabitants of which had deserted it.[26] I encamped my small party with the store of ammunition in a garden, and took up my quarters in a sort of summer-house, remaining for ten days, when, to my no small satisfaction, I received orders from the general officer in command at Neeza to re-join my regiment.

---

not think it worth providing a fuller account of this action, as the Light Division played a significant role in it.

25 In the aftermath of Fuentes de Oñoro, Wellington departed for the southern theatre along with the Third and Seventh Divisions. The Light Division remained as part of a northern covering force under Lt. General Sir Brent Spencer to observe the movements of the Armée du Portugal, and when that force, now under Marshal Marmont, marched south to link up with Soult's Armée du Midi Spencer's corps followed them south. This march, however, took place in the first weeks of June 1811, not in July as Hay says.

26 Nisa, a town in the Alentejo, some thirty miles east of Abrantes.

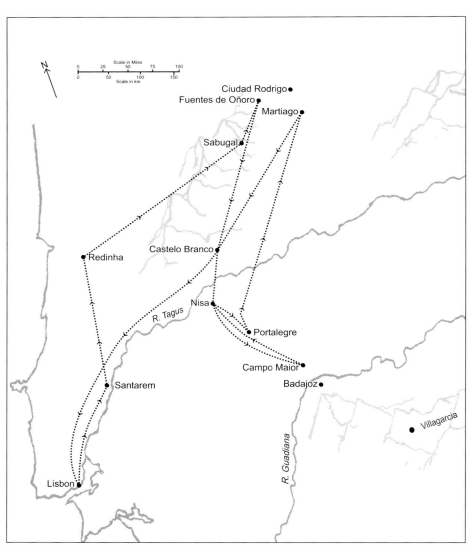

Map 1 Hay in the Peninsula 1810-1811.

I should here mention that on our return from the south to the north our route was in some degree changed from the one we had marched by some months before. When we arrived at a considerable town, called Portalegre, instead of continuing on the main road towards the Tagus, we were ordered to proceed by mountain passes to a very beautifully situated town, called Castel de Vieda, where it was Lord Wellington's intention the Light Division should repose from the great fatigues which they had of late under-gone, for as long as the movements of the French would admit.[27]

The distance between Portalegre and Castel de Vieda may not exceed fifteen English miles – if as much – but at least one half the distance had to be travelled by passes up and down the sides of steep mountains, not safe to ride over, even on the surefooted mules and asses of the country; and where roads were made in the valley, they were hurriedly paved with large rough stones to make them at all passable in the wet weather. At the time of our marching the weather was extremely hot, and it was after a day of extreme fatigue that we reached our destined quarters, situated on the summit of a very high hill, or, rather, mountain.

The French not having been at Castel de Vieda, we found the town in much better order than any of those we had been in the habit of living in during our marches up and down the country.

General Sir Robert Crawford [sic – Craufurd],[28] who then commanded our division, was not a man to allow idle habits, however, so immediately on our reaching these better quarters he issued orders that the full regulations of attending garrison parades, guard mounting, and marching out every morning to exercise the men should be carried out during our stay at Castel de Vieda. Accordingly, next morning we were marched out about five miles from the town before sunrise; there we halted, arms were piled, and we officers collected in groups and enjoyed ourselves lying about on the grass.

Among the topics discussed was the dreadful march of the day before, the dangerous state of the hillsides to ride up and down, etc., when I happened to remark, half jokingly, I would rather march it again than mount guard that day. (It took the division eight hours to perform the distance of fifteen miles which will give you some idea of the road.) Upon my saying this some of my companions asked how long I would take to go to Portalegre and back? I said I would undertake to do it in two hours and a half on a certain mare, a little Portuguese animal I had at that time in my possession. Many voices exclaimed, 'Impossible!' Amongst them was that of my old friend of walking celebrity at Ashford, Lieutenant Kerr, he

---

27   The town is in fact Castelo de Vide. Situated, as the crow flies, some ten miles north of Portalegre, the distance by road, as Hay relates, was and is somewhat further.

28   As well as misspelling his late general's name, Hay also errs in creating him a knight. His rank at this time was major general.

offered to bet immediately against my undertaking, which was accepted by some one.

My intended ride soon got round, and a lively excitement was created in the division, particularly among the sporting characters, of whom there were a good many. Bets were made to considerable amounts against my being able to accomplish my task, as high as thirty to one against either me or the mare singly, and fifteen and twenty to one against us both – a large amount of opinion against mine!

However, an umpire was appointed – Captain Rorke of the 52nd – and on our return to the town, it was agreed he should be despatched two hours before me to witness my arrival in the Market Place of Portalegre.[29] I never bet, but on this occasion I did go to the length of half a £5 note with a brother officer, who had backed me, rather for the honour of our corps than with any hope of my success.

I got my breakfast, the mare was fed and led out to be looked at, as the troops had assembled for parade and guard mounting. The day was extremely hot, and many tried to persuade me to relinquish my intention, amongst them that most kind and amiable man who commanded our brigade, Major [sic] Drummond.[30] I told him I had gone too far on account of the bets of others, and if he would kindly give me leave to be absent from my quarters for two and a half hours, I would promise, if my life was spared, to be back in that time. His reply was his best wishes for my success, and he most considerately insisted on my accepting the loan of his stop-watch.

I started at a gentle trot; the first four miles were through a plain on a rough, badly paved road, I then had to commence the ascent of a mountain which I found steep in places beyond even what I myself could have believed possible. However, I gained the top without distressing my mare, and down the other side I went trusting to the sure-footed animal I rode; I soon gained the plain, ascended and descended the second mountain; but the little mare was beginning to show signs of distress from the great heat of the sun. I was within about four miles of Portalegre when I overtook the umpire, who could not believe I had waited the two hours agreed upon before starting, as he said he had ridden fast the whole way and he desired me to proceed, and, as a guarantee, to go up to the Market Place and read the first two lines of any proclamation that might be stuck up there and tell him the words on my return.

The road was now between two high walls, and what at first I considered a misfortune afterwards proved to be in both my own and the mare's favour, it was crowded by commissariat mules loaded with bags and barrels. Seeing this

---

29   The identity of this officer is a mystery: Challis lists no-one of that name, or anything like it, as serving in the Peninsular army let alone the 52nd.

30   The brigade commander at this time was Brigadier General George Duncan Drummond, late of the 24th Foot. It is unclear why his rank is given as 'major', unless in error for major general: Drummond, however, never achieved the latter rank, dying of illness on 8 September 1811 when still a brigadier general on the staff with the substantive rank of colonel.

I dismounted in despair by a stream, into which I dipped my handkerchief and wiped the poor mare's nostrils, and then looked for the first time at the general's watch. This, and the necessary slackening of pace to enable us to pass the mules, quite refreshed my animal, and jostling and working we got through the living obstruction and entered the narrow streets of the town; here I met officers of the first division quartered there, all anxious for news from the outposts. I did not stop to answer, however, but rode straight on to the Market Place, and read some Proclamation of the Authorities, returning as I came.

Again I dismounted at the brook and washed my own and the mare's face; but when I arrived at the last mountain I felt myself almost exhausted and my poor animal nearly spent; indeed, to keep her from falling, I had to throw the weight of my body from side to side as we began to descend the last hill.

Turning my eyes to some trees at a little distance, I saw a man just in the act of mounting his horse; he turned out to be my friend Kerr, who, having bet such large sums against me, was most anxious about the result. On seeing me he exclaimed: 'What! Have you given up?' All the mare needed, I knew, was a stimulus to rouse her mettle for the rest of the distance; I therefore said I would tell him all about it if he would ride beside me, and the mare, having a horse alongside her, seemed to forget her fatigue and rushed on; thus we reached the gate within the time – having indeed six minutes to spare! I was received with loud cheers, taken off the mare's back by the men of my company, and carried on their shoulders to my quarters, where I was very glad to lie down.

A few days longer stay in this place was all we were allowed, as, from some unforeseen movement on the part of the French army, we received sudden orders to march, and in two days reached the little town of Neeza, where, as I have already mentioned, I was left behind with a small detachment. I did not tell you that while marching from there to return to my regiment, my astonished eyes first beheld four wolves feeding on a dead horse.

My men were all fine, tried soldiers, as anxious as I was to push on to the front, and it was at their request I consented to double our marches and encamp where we found it most convenient for the night, always starting long before daybreak, halting for a few hours during the heat of the day, and on again till dark.

On our way we had to cross the Tagus where the country on either side was wild, wretched, and uncultivated, covered with thickets and a wild shrub, called Gumcistus, and through which wolves followed the army in actual flocks.[31] I had started by myself at the head of my party, when I came suddenly on four fierce animals; my appearance did not even cause them to relinquish their repast; but I was glad when my men came up, and, taking a sergeant's musket, I fired a shot,

31 Gumcistus, or gum cistus, is the common name applied to resin-bearing species of the family Cistaceae (commonly known as rockroses), especially *Cistus ladanifer* which is native to the Western Mediterranean.

which, however, only had the effect of making them retreat for a few moments till we passed.

It was during this march I was congratulated by Major – now Colonel – Rowan (my present chief and first Commissioner of Police) who said, 'I congratulate you Hay, on your promotion'; I naturally thought he alluded to my having succeeded to the vacant lieutenancy of the 52nd, to which I was entitled; and, on his telling me he meant the 12th Light Dragoons, I treated the matter as a jest, it being such an utterly unexpected piece of good luck, I could only think he was quizzing me; at which he was somewhat offended.[32]

On reaching my regiment, I found, to my surprise and delight, the news was true; my brother officers congratulating me on seeing my name in the *Gazette*. My commission was dated: Lieutenant, 12th Light Dragoons, June 11, 1811.[33]

As we were marching in such extremely hot weather, we rested at noon, starting again later on. One afternoon we had to witness an act of diabolical tyranny. On the road was a stream of considerable depth, up to a man's middle; over this river was a bridge. Our general, commanding the division, considering it more cooling and refreshing for the men, took his own post on the bridge with his staff, and directed the first division to march through the water. The first division had passed, and was about three miles in advance. The general, from his position on the bridge, observed two or three of the 95th take some water in their hands to cool their parched mouths; instantly the halt was sounded, the brigade ordered to retrace their steps, the whole division formed into hollow square, and these unfortunate men paraded, stripped, and flogged. Such scenes, alas! were of almost daily occurrence, and disgusted me beyond measure. About this time Lieutenant-Colonel Ross left the regiment on leave, and was succeeded by Major Gibbs in temporary command.[34] I had in every way received the most considerate kindness from Colonel Ross, and felt truly and deeply affected at his leaving; indeed, his loss could only have been made up for by the excellent, gentlemanly, and kind-hearted man who succeeded him.

Each day was now bringing us nearer the French; and at last we came to their rear-guard, at a place called Fort Grenaldie, driving them before us as usual.[35] On one of these occasions, our day's work being over, my kind friend Major Gibbs,

---

32 This was Charles Rowan, recently (9 May 1811) promoted to major in the 52nd, in which he had served as a captain since 1803. He served for the remainder of the Peninsular War, chiefly in staff positions, and at Waterloo where he was wounded, ending the war as a brevet lieutenant colonel. He was appointed Senior Commissioner of London Metropolitan Police in 1829, on the recommendation of the Duke of Wellington.

33 The date of Hay's promotion was in fact 11 June 1811.

34 Ross in fact left the regiment in order to assume the post of Deputy Adjutant General in Ceylon, for which purpose he exchanged into the 66th Foot, the first battalion of which formed part of the garrison of that island.

35 Hay presumably here means Fuente Guinaldo, although there was no serious fighting there at this time.

said to me: 'Hay, I do think it rather hard you should continue to be needlessly exposed to this business when you actually do not belong to the regiment.' Then added: 'If you like, I will speak to General Crawford [sic] to allow you to report yourself to the 12th [Light] Dragoons, whose encampment we shall pass through this evening.'

Although I felt in no hurry to leave my old companions, with whom I was so happy, still, the temptation to a poor walking ensign to become the owner of a charger at once and to enjoy the comparative comforts of a cavalry regiment, such as the 12th then had, just fresh from England, with new outfits, while we were in rags, was too much to be resisted, and the major kindly took his opportunity to make his request. The reply was very different from that which he had a right to expect, either as a commanding officer, or from his own just and honourable notions of the service. However, his only observation to me was, 'I shall ask no more from General Crawford [sic],' and that I must continue to do my duty with the 52nd until officially transferred. I am certain I did not feel half so much mortified at hearing the result of his application as he did in making it known to me!

We had reached the frontiers of Spain and driven the enemy under the walls of Ciudad Rodrigo; our regiment occupied a village called Montagua for a few days after our arrival, to enable us to become well acquainted with the neighbourhood.[36] For these few days we remained quiet, turning out every morning on the alarm ground, two hours before daylight, and returning after ten o'clock to our quarters; but, before long, orders were given to commence making preparations for the siege of Ciudad Rodrigo; certain companies were to be employed as working parties – breaking ground, making fascines, gabions, etc.

One morning, when leaving parade, my good friend the major beckoned me to him; all he said was, 'Hay! You are well mounted, the 12th are quartered about thirty miles from this. I will not enquire after you until daylight tomorrow, and, by the way, Lord Combermere's headquarters are halfway between us, and he is senior to General Crawford [sic].'[37]

I took the hint, and, with a nod of delight, thanked my truly kind friend and was off like a shot to make preparations. I knew it would be necessary to make some one my confidant as I could not furnish coin enough from my own exchequer to meet even a shilling extra expense; but as we lived on the most brotherly terms, the fellow comrade, to whom I mentioned my proposed excursion, immediately suggested accompanying me and paying all expenses if I would only lend him a horse. I had at that time my famous little mare that had previously won the match against time, and another very clever little horse; I, therefore, most willingly

---

36 Martiago, situated 13 miles south of Ciudad Rodrigo and headquarters of the Light Division at this time.

37 Hay is clearly here remembering with advantage; the commander of Wellington's cavalry was Lt. General Sir Stapleton Cotton, but he would not be ennobled as Lord Combermere until 1814.

consented, if he could get the major's leave. An hour settled that and all other arrangements, and we left the cantonment for the headquarters of the 12th Light Dragoons. The road was very rough with some steep hills and mountains and streams to pass; but towards noon without any adventure we reached the quarters of Lord Combermere. I saw Lord James Hay, his *aide-de-camp*, who undertook to have ready for me on my return an order from his lordship, as commander-in-chief of the cavalry to join my regiment, on his obtaining from the commanding officer of the 12th a requisition to that effect.[38] I found, on reaching the villages where I had been told the 12th were quartered, that they had moved ten miles further in advance.

Sad news this for me also for our horses, both requiring rest and nourishment. However, I was determined nothing should now stop me from obtaining my interview with the officer in command. About three o'clock we made out the village where the headquarters were.[39] There I made myself and my mission known to Major Wyndham, and was most kindly received and the tender of my services to join my corps fully appreciated.[40] My brother officers, to be, were very civil and anxious for us to remain and rest ourselves and our much-tired animals for the night, but the temptation I firmly declined, as I had given my promise to Major Gibbs to be on the alarm post of the Light Division at daybreak.

A letter was duly written by Major Wyndham to the commander-in-chief of the cavalry; we and our horses well fed; and we were once more *en route* for Montagua. But one should always remember the old saying, 'There's many a slip,' etc.; it was evening by the time we reached the headquarters of Lord Combermere. I delivered my despatch and received my answer in due form, with leave of absence for three months to enable me to equip myself for dragoon service. Being light in weight as well as spirits I could, in those days, undergo a great deal of fatigue both in body

---

38   This was Lieutenant and Captain Lord James Hay, 1st Foot Guards. Having initially served in the Peninsula with the 2/52nd during the Coruna campaign he subsequently served as an aide to lieutenant generals Sherbrooke and Cotton, remaining on the latter's staff until the end of the war. Later served at Waterloo and was a full general by the time of his death in 1862. As a son of the 7th Marquis of Tweeddale, he was a very distant relation to William Hay.

39   The Monthly Returns for the 12th Light Dragoons (TNA, WO17/35) place the regiment at 'Nave' – presumably Nave de Haver on the old Fuentes de Oñoro battlefield – on 25 August and at Fuente Guinaldo on 25 September. The distance from Martiago to Nave de Haver is somewhat over thirty miles by road but around that as the crow flies, whereas Fuente Guinaldo is rather closer. Unless the regiment moved again during the period between these returns, it is likely that it was to the latter that Hay rode in the first instance before being obliged to partially retrace his steps.

40   The temporary commanding officer of the 12th Light Dragoons, pending the arrival of Lt. Colonel the Hon. Frederick Ponsonby, was Major George Wyndham. Son of the 3rd Earl of Egremont, Wyndham was a recent arrival in the regiment and had left it again by February 1812. By all accounts he was an ineffective officer, something which owed at least a little to his flitting from regiment to regiment in order to further his career. See Andrew Bamford, *Gallantry and Discipline: The 12th Light Dragoons at War With Wellington* (Barnsley: Frontline, 2014), pp.35-36, 134-137.

and mind, and, though I had ridden upwards of seventy miles, I was still fresh; not so with my fellow traveller, he and his pony would fain have rested that night at the cavalry headquarters, but to this I would not agree, so on we went!

It had become nearly dark, and our way was over an uncultivated plain covered with large rocks, and with many roads leading in all directions. Amongst these we soon became confused; I was a little in advance, when I thought I saw some one pass quickly across the road before me, on horseback carrying a lance. I pulled up and waited for my companion, asking if he had seen anything. He said 'No.' In a few moments, and while we were still speaking, I saw two more figures pass in the same manner. I asked if he saw these, his answer, from hunger and fatigue, was rather short, and he enquired if I were dreaming. Hardly were the words out of his mouth, when we were surrounded by about a dozen ill-looking fellows, with their lances pointed towards us, demanding us to stand and surrender ourselves prisoners.

We were in no condition to dispute the point, but enquired who and what they were. The answer was 'Spanish Guerillas!' We told them who we were, whence from, and where going, but of no avail; it was insisted that we were deserters going over to the French, so we were marched off about two miles to where was their chief and another party. On showing him my papers, and explaining who we were, he became very civil, and said we had mistaken the road, and were going, at the

'A distant view of Ciudad Rodrigo… with a troop of Spanish guerrillas': Aquatint by Chares Turner after Thomas St Clair. (Anne S.K. Brown Military Collection)

time his men stopped us, straight into the French lines, having in the darkness got in advance of all British outposts. The chief gave us in charge of two of his men with orders to conduct us to a certain miller's house in a small hamlet near the river where, he said, it was absolutely necessary for our safety to remain all night.

Perforce I had no remedy, so to the miller's care we were consigned, our horses taken from us, and we were shut into a small room like a hole in the wall. No light was allowed and we were told to keep very quiet, as the French patrols passed the place frequently in the night. One may generally place perfect confidence in the honour of a Spaniard if he undertake the care of your person or goods, therefore we did so, although in this case there was no alternative!

A large mess of bread and milk was brought for our supper, and, after having discussed this, I threw myself down and slept as soundly as ever in my life till I was roused about 5 a.m. by the miller, to say we must be off without delay as the patrols had just returned and the coast was clear, and our guides and, horses were waiting at a certain gate he pointed out. If the French had found out that this man had concealed English officers in his house, his fate and that of his family and property were sealed; notwithstanding this he was quite offended at our offering him some small remuneration for his hospitality both towards ourselves and our ponies.

We took our leave and, preceded by a tall Spaniard rolled in his cloak and with a long stick in his hand, made our way towards the river by most rugged paths; when we reached the banks of the Douro, which we had passed the morning before with but little water in it, what was our horror and astonishment to find a perfect torrent roaring down amongst the great rocks which formed the bed of the mountain stream![41] Fording it was out of the question, but our guide who, from the rain in the night, had expected such a state of things, said he knew of a dam to which he could take us by another route; this dam, or causeway, made a perfect Fall of Niagara in miniature. It must have been about one hundred and fifty yards long by one and a half broad, paved with large flat stones, and the chasm over which the water fell must have been over one hundred feet deep. It was fearful to look at, the water, which, at the moment we came up to it, was at least two and a half feet deep rushing over the flat platform.

My friend, almost paralysed with astonishment, remonstrated; but I saw there was nothing else for it but to take our chance, or my word to my commanding officer was forfeited; consequently, I ordered the guide to proceed at once, which he did, supporting himself with his sharp pointed stick to prevent being carried off his legs by the force of the water. When about halfway across, my eyes steadily fixed on the opposite shore, I heard the cries of my companion for help, as his pony would stop to drink and his own head was swimming. It was impossible to turn round – so his getting out of the difficulty was entirely providential, and no credit to us.

41   The river cannot have been the Douro, which runs some forty miles further north, and was most likely the Água, which flows northwards to meet the Douro near Barca de Alva.

The rocks on the opposite side gained, our guide paid, and dismissed, our spurs were driven well into the flanks of my poor horses, and the division was just moving from the alarm posts as I rode up to my good friend Major Gibbs. He received me with his wonted kindness, and said no apology was needed for being a few moments late for parade; indeed, he added, when he gave me leave to make the trial, he did not expect it would be possible for me to perform what I had done under two days and he did not intend to enquire after me until after three days' absence.

Lord Combermere's letters made General Crawford relinquish his hold of me, and preparations were made for my departure and little arrangements entered into with my brother officers, among whom I had lived so happily. I felt quite sorry for my good luck when the time really had come that I must separate from them all. What few dollars one, more fortunate than the rest, had collected were furnished me for my journey to Lisbon, in exchange for a draft on England.

My uniform, etc., was divided among my messmates, and one officer, being greatly in need of a pair of 'Rifle Wings' and having no money, offered me his Portuguese servant-boy. He was an active, neat, intelligent lad and the very thing I most wanted, so that bargain was struck, and with this lad and my two ponies I took my departure from the 52nd on my journey of three hundred miles to Lisbon, through an almost deserted country, infested by stragglers from the Army and desperate characters belonging to the unfortunate country people who had been driven from their homes in the mountains.

I cannot conclude this first stage of my career, as I may call it, without a parenthetic remark or two.

I commenced my military duties at so early an age, I had not forgotten that obedience and respect were due to superior rank and station, especially to the officers under whose command chance had placed me; consequently, I followed their instructions and formed no ideas of my own, such obedience and the feeling of having no responsibility, save as to the fulfilment of my superiors' wishes to the best of my ability, had been most conducive to my happiness and, to the time I left the 52nd – to join the 12th [Light] Dragoons – I had lived as a child in a happy and well-conducted family, for, at the time I write of, nothing could exceed the mutual kindliness of feeling which existed in that most estimable corps. Such a feeling as selfishness did not exist, and probably accounted for this excellent state of things; a stranger, entering with a different disposition, soon found himself so much out of place, that he did not remain long in the regiment.

During the twelve months I had been in the regiment I had learnt – most practically – the rudiments of a soldier's life, including long marches in hot and wet weather, seldom during the whole time sleeping under any canopy but heaven, nearly always with clothes on; and last, but not least, having been engaged in fourteen or fifteen actions and skirmishes – that is in everything that took place between the battle of Busaco and the siege of Ciudad Rodrigo.

Contemplating these facts, and remembering I was suddenly starting on a new life, parting from friends and advisers, many of whom, from the chance of war, I might never see again, I passed sadly, the first few miles of my journey over a ragged road at a slow pace.

It was one of the gifts bestowed on me by Nature to reflect deeply and decide quickly, on this occasion it was necessary for me to do so; there were two lines of march, diverging from the spot I had now reached – one, the northern, the other, the southern road to Lisbon; the former we had fought our way up by, during the retreat of Massena from Santarem, this route I knew well: a dreary, desolate path, towns and villages burnt down, inhabitants murdered, fields uncultivated, truly an uninviting journey alone, with but a young boy-servant. The southern line the French had been by but little and the inhabitants had returned or were returning to their homes in some of the towns.

Little or no fighting had taken place between the two armies, and, although some forty or fifty miles farther, I decided to take this line.

Francisco – my servant – was mounted on a pony carrying a pair of light wicker panniers, containing a very limited quantity of clothing and a ham, in case we could procure no other provisions. I rode the other pony, and by travelling late and early, making long marches each day, we got over the ground wonderfully well, without any adventure until we arrived at a considerable town called Castello Branco, about halfway; there I found a sort of depôt for sick and wounded soldiers, and the medical officer, an excellent fellow whom I had known before, invited me most pressingly to stay with him a few days to rest myself and ponies.

Being really in need of repose, I consented, and the time passed so pleasantly, I began to forget I had half a long journey still before me, and a considerable portion of my leave had expired, when a sudden disturbance – the result of my own indiscretion – not only made me glad to move quickly on my route to Lisbon, but nearly cost me my life, and that not in a way that would have entitled me to honourable mention in the *Gazette*!

Upstairs was reserved for the owner's family which was never seen, nor did any of us know of what it consisted, the only member of it, who ever appeared, being an antiquated grandee, dressed in a costume of a hundred years ago, who sometimes in the evening walked in his garden, but had no intercourse with the heretic soldiers. At the side of the house grew a very large mulberry-tree, and I often amused myself by climbing into it and sitting on a branch to eat the fruit. Having one evening climbed higher than before, I was able to see distinctly into the windows of the upper part of the house; from one of these I was soon observed by a pretty, black eyed girl; I made signs to her and she soon came closer to the window and we began to talk. After a little conversation she asked me to come and see her, no doubt little thinking I would act on her invitation at once; but this I did, I hurried down the tree and upstairs into the room which, from its position, I guessed to be the one in which I had seen her; to my amazement I found, on opening the door, I was in a large gallery hung with portraits, and seated round the room on the floor were a number of women, some old and some, as far as my astonished eyes could discover, young.

On my abrupt entrance the most awful yell was given by the whole party; at the same moment a door, I had not observed, it being covered with tapestry, was flung open and the little old grandee rushed at me sword in hand; a few strides at 'double-quick' (in taking which I nearly knocked down the girl who had first caused the disturbance, and who now appeared on the scene by the same door I had entered, calling 'murder,' as loudly as any of the party) brought me into the doctor's room below. He was thunderstruck by my discoveries, and we were laughing at my adventures when my boy entered and informed us he had discovered it was the intention of our kindly host to have my life for having invaded the presence of his ladies. He and a priest, who visited him, had determined to watch my movements and – unknown to any of us – stab me! The girl who had been the cause of the mischief, having overheard their conversation had sent me this warning, beseeching me to save my life by flight. The doctor soon discovered the information was quite correct, for the old gentleman demanded an audience and in his rage let out his intention of killing me that night; therefore, to save him that trouble, I was on the road to Lisbon before another hour was over, arriving there after another week's ride.

Having, as best I could, cleaned myself and clothes, I waited on the commandant, presenting the introduction I had received from the Marquis of Tweeddale.[42] Here a new chapter in my life begins. I found the commandant most kind and hospitable; he recommended me to tailors, saddlers, etc., for my outfit, and supplied me with chargers at his own price, for an infantry officer could not be expected to know anything about horses by a cavalry commandant!

Hitherto I had been accustomed to hard work in one of the very best disciplined regiments in the service, I now found myself nearly my own master. No parades, no drills, no alarm post an hour before daylight. I was astonished at the difference between dragoon life at a depôt and light infantry life at the outposts, and I was soldier enough at heart to prefer the latter; so, after a short stay and a great deal of asking, I at last succeeded in obtaining leave to join my regiment on the frontiers; but that was easier said than done. The many privations and great fatigues I had undergone, added to the present wet season, and the total change in my habits since coming to Lisbon, had, almost unknown to myself, injured my health; so a few days after my departure with the detachment I began to feel seriously unwell, my head and limbs ached, and I could scarcely drag myself along, until we reached the garrison town of Abrantes where there was a hospital station.

On arriving there, at the end of a day's march, I threw myself down in my cloak on the ground till my servant came up with the baggage; he at once started to find a doctor, who pronounced me to be in a high fever, very ill, and quite unfit

42   The commandant at Lisbon at this time was Major General Warren Peacocke.

to proceed another step. For two or three days, perhaps more, I lay almost uncon-scious and quite indifferent to my fate; but when I began to recover and found myself left behind, I was in true distress of mind; however, the medical man, far from allowing me to proceed, insisted that I must return to Lisbon, as it would be some weeks, at least, till I was fit for duty.

The only mode by which I could be moved was by water, on board one of the large flat-bottomed boats used for carrying provisions for the Army, and returning laden with sick and wounded. On the one in which I was placed I found a party of highlanders; and among them one of the finest and bravest of all men it was ever my lot to meet, Colonel Cameron of the 79th, going to Lisbon himself on sick leave.[43] He took a lively interest in me and showed me very great sympathy and attention in my helpless state.

After a most tedious progress, running aground, etc., etc., in the course of three or four days we reached the landing-steps of the Black Horse Square, Lisbon. Utterly disappointed and miserable, I reported myself to the commandant and medical officer, and found myself officially on the sick list for the first time in my soldier's life, but, being disposed by nature to make light of ailments, and having a good constitution, under the able attention of Dr. Hossack, I soon began to recover and look about for work.[44]

At that time nearly all the officers had been sent off with fresh mounts to join the Army, leaving a great number of privates of doubtful character, and lame and sick horses to be looked after, and very few to do it. Though not sufficiently recovered to do much I tendered my services for this duty. There were so many sick, and the doctor's hands so full, that my escaping his care and exchanging my billet without consulting him were never enquired into; and the consequence of the work I had undertaken being too much for me, was a relapse of fever, which nearly proved fatal. I was ill at least a month – the greater part of the time delirious. When I considered myself sufficiently recovered from my second attack I obtained a promise from the commandant to allow me to accompany the first detachment, as I felt certain I should never be well till once more with my regiment on active service. On the strength of this promise I had ordered my servant to make preparations: horses shod, etc.; when one morning the sergeant of my regiment came to me to tell me the new colonel, appointed to the 12th Dragoons, had arrived from England the night before and wished to see me. (This officer was the Hon. Frederick Ponsonby of whom as I proceed I shall have to make frequent honourable mention.)[45] I at

---

43   There would seem to be some confusion here, as there was no 'Colonel Cameron of the 79th' serving in the Peninsula at this time: most likely the officer meant is Lt. Colonel John Cameron of Fassiefern, who was then commanding the 1/92nd. Hay has presumably confused the surname and the regiment, the 79th being the Cameron Highlanders.

44   This was Staff Surgeon James Hosack, previously Assistant Surgeon of the 2/23rd.

45   Lt. Colonel the Hon. Frederick Cavendish Ponsonby commanded the 12th Light Dragoons in the Peninsula from September 1811 until the end of the war, except for some months in late 1811 and early

once started for the colonel's quarters; arrived there he asked me all about the men and horses at the depôt, and many more questions, as to when I was going to join, etc. On my telling him I was to proceed with a detachment in the course of a week, he said: 'Surely that cannot be, you are not in a fit state of health.' The fact is at that time, with the aid of a stick in each hand, I was just able to crawl, certainly not walk; but, as at that time I had no beard to shave and rarely saw myself in a glass, I had no idea how ill I looked.

The colonel, however, seemed quite struck with my appearance; he sat down and wrote a few lines which he gave to his servant, who in a few moments returned accompanied by my former friend Dr. Hossack; Colonel Ponsonby asked if he had been attending me; the doctor seemed confounded to see me in such a state, and said he had, but I had withdrawn myself from his care and the sick-list long ago, and where I had gone to, he could never make out. I explained my motives and the lack of officers, but was told that would not do, I was quite unfit for duty; and all I could say before the doctor was of little avail as he only shook his head at me, and it ended by my being ordered to appear before a medical board in an hour from that time. I was by them pronounced in a very bad state, and told I had leave of absence for three months to proceed to England, that the packet sailed for Falmouth that afternoon, and in her I must go! At that I remonstrated, the duke's leave must first be obtained,[46] I said, but the reply of the board was, 'Their certificate would bear me harmless and go I must.' My health was such from my own neglect, and Dr. Hossack would not be any further responsible. I therefore had no alternative but to crawl back to my lodgings and make hasty preparations for my departure.[47]

My camp equipage and horses I had to leave to the mercy of a person whose name I will not mention, as he had professed great friendship for me, and is now dead – suffice it to say I lost all my property entrusted to his care. During my stay at Belham [sic – Belém], after my return sick from Abrantes, and which may have been some five or six weeks or more, I was at first too ill, and latterly too occupied to write home, hence no letters had been sent to my mother since before I was taken ill the first time, when I had written to say I had got my horses and uniform,

---

1812 when he was acting as a brigade commander in the absence of Major General Anson. As such, he will feature frequently in the remainder of Hay's narrative. Although Hay is correct in saying that he was newly-arrived in Portugal when the two men met at Lisbon, this was in consequence of his having been in Britain on sick-leave: he had previously served in the Peninsula from June 1809 to April 1811 first as a major in the 23rd Light Dragoons and then, when that regiment went home after Talavera, as a staff officer.

46 Hay is here again using titles that had not yet been conferred; Wellington was not at this stage a duke but rather a viscount.

47 Possibly as a result of this sudden and irregular departure, Hay was for some months listed as absent without leave in the Monthly Returns of the 12th Light Dragoons during early 1812 before news reached the regiment that he had been sent back to Britain.

and was to join in a few days and would not write again till after my arrival with my regiment, therefore no uneasiness had been felt at home at my silence.

I started from Lisbon in the month of December, in the *Elizabeth* packet, several officers, proceeding to England on leave of absence, being my fellow passengers. After a most stormy and rough passage of nearly three weeks, we landed at Falmouth. In those days it took several days to reach London from Cornwall; arrived there I went, by advice of one of my ship companions, to the Craven Hotel, Strand, where, as I had no dress but my dragoon uniform in which to appear, I attracted considerable notice; and my sickly appearance caused the landlady to show me much kindness and attention. I gave my tailor a day in which to furnish me with a travelling-suit, and once more took the road per mail-coach for Scotland.

The English mail arrived in those days at Dunbar about 8 p.m., there I took a postchaise and proceeded to my paternal home, Spott. The room usually occupied by the family was at the back part of the dear old house, and from its distance from the front, no sound of an arrival could be heard; hence no one met me as I drove to the door, and it is difficult to describe my feelings and emotions, as, running up to it never thinking of ringing or knocking, I opened it and walked in direct to the back drawing-room, in which I found all who were dearest to me in the world, just as I had left them before my campaigns began.

Conceive their astonishment, and the exclamation of the whole party 'William!' – I hear it now in my ears – when I put in my head! My poor father alone remained unmoved and uttered no sound. A dread had flashed across his mind, that I had got into some scrape or trouble and been sent home in disgrace. A very short explanation, however, together with my worn and sickly appearance, soon showed why I was there, and every care and kindness, that the most affectionate of parents and sisters could bestow, was lavished upon me.

With their nursing and the doctoring of old Trumble, the family medical man, I soon began to improve in health; and as I did so, my greatest anxiety, from my restless spirit, was to get back to my regiment and to active service, as my being at home when my comrades were employed in the field, did not suit my ideas of a soldier.

The only remains of my illness was a tedious ague with slight fever, which came on every other day at the same hour regularly, in spite of all Trumble's nostrums.

My kind father wished to procure for me a longer leave; but all persuasions had no effect on my mind. I would return to my work, consequently his next care was to provide me with a good and faithful servant, good horses, and all possible comforts he could think of, for I was still very young – only eighteen – though I had been engaged in at least ten different fights already, and had undergone such great fatigue.

2

With the 12th Light Dragoons in the Peninsula

I left my dear family and home once more in the March of 1812, and departed from London to join the depôt of the 12th, then quartered at Radipol[e] barracks, near Weymouth, where I found it necessary to stay a few days to furnish myself with appointments, etc.[1]

It was on the day of my arrival in town that Mr. Percival, the then Prime Minister, was shot, entering the House of Commons – an event which caused a great sensation at the time.[2]

From London I repaired to Dorsetshire and joined the depôt; I found there a set of young men up to all kinds of amusements and pranks, in which I joined, for, being free from restraint, I had little care for my health, which was still precarious; indeed, on one occasion I was taken so ill after a night ride of fifty miles on coast-guard duty – at that time entrusted to the military authorities – that I had to be

---

1   The depot of the 12th Light Dragoons, composed of four troops, was stationed at Radipole Barracks from September 1811. The depots of other light cavalry units serving in the Peninsula were also consolidated at this location, and remained there until shifted to Dorchester in August 1813. See Bamford, *Gallantry and Discipline*, p.119. Particularly considering the date he subsequently gives for his arrival at Radipole, Hay's dating here may be a little off. On 2 April, General Sir James Steuart, regimental colonel of the 12th Light Dragoons, had written to Major Wyndham as follows: 'Capt. Clark being the youngest Captain and having been so long sick, should in my opinion be called home and replaced by Wallace who should take command of the Remount to go out, and Clark to join the Depot at Weymouth. Lieutenants Hall, Carew and Isherwood having sent in their resignations on account of ill health Lieutenants Arnold, Goldsmid and Calderwood should also be ordered out with the Remount. Lieut. Hay's health not being yet perfectly established had better be ordered to join the depot at Weymouth when his present leave expires and Pinfold ordered out in his room. If you have no objection to this arrangement you may use my authority for having it carried into effect and make the necessary application accordingly to the Adjutant General'. Steuart to Wyndham, 2 April 1812, 9th/12th Royal Lancers Regimental Museum, Derby, 912L:2088/44 "Letterbook of Col. Stewart [sic] 1806-1818".

2   This took place on 11 May 1812. Hay's arrival on that date would tend to confirm the assumption noted above that his leave expired some time in April and that he received his orders for the depot at that point.

bled by the sergeant of my troop to save my life, and the doctor who came in the morning said it was the right thing to do. My servant was horrified at the amount of blood-letting, but the sergeant said it was no use unless he bled me till I fainted, which, sure enough, he did.

General Jones, of the 18th Hussars, a great martinet, at this time commanded the district.[3] I, in consequence of my drilling in the good old 52nd, being attentive to my duties, became a favourite with him, which led him to notice the delicate state of my health.

One morning, the post having brought an order for all officers, men, and horses able to move, to be sent forthwith to join their respective corps in Spain, I was horrified to find my name omitted from orders in the evening.

I immediately waited on the commanding officer to find out the cause of the mistake, as such, I, of course, thought it must be; but he told me it was no mistake but an order from General Jones, that my name should be taken from the list submitted to him of those to join, as neither he, nor the medical man consid-ered my health sufficiently reinstated to leave the country. On this I proceeded to the general's quarters, but could get no satisfactory reply from him then; but next morning, when inspecting the men and horses selected, he called me out of the ranks, and said he fully appreciated the motives that prompted me to wish to join my regiment, but he and the doctor considered me quite unfit, and offered me a year's leave to go home. But I refused all advances, and said I would far rather take my chance, and, indeed, urged my claim so hard that he gave way, adding I was 'An obstinate fellow to be so bent on my own death,' with a few other complimentary words, when I made my escape from him delighted at having attained my object.

We, who were bound for the seat of war, soon took our leave of Radipol[e] and by different detachments marched to Portsmouth for embarkation. The only adventure I nearly had on this occasion happened at Ringwood, on the borders of the New Forest. We arrived at this town on Saturday evening, and 'on the march' Sunday is a halt-day. While lounging about the innyard, I made myself acquainted with the landlord, who, I soon discovered, professed to be a sportsman, but was in reality a regular deer-killer in the New Forest, if it suited his purpose. I quickly improved the opportunity with my friendly host and not only did he show me his dogs, but after a little persuasion, consented to let me see a deer killed next morning. He knew we were on our way to embark, and that his risk of being informed against was slight; all was soon arranged; I was to get the officer in command to march as early as possible, so as to admit of myself and companions – all of whom, when told, were delighted at the fun and the idea of adding a buck to the provision for the voyage – meeting our

---

3   This was Major General Oliver Jones, who, as a lieutenant colonel, had previously commanded the 18th Hussars in Portugal in 1808 and in the Coruna Campaign.

host at a certain fixed spot just before daybreak. This we did, and a lovely morning it was.

Carbines had been borrowed from the troopers' saddles, and the host's two handsome lurchers given in charge of our servants; the innkeeper himself keeping well out of sight, after having pointed out to us where the deer were to be found feeding. Sure enough, on reaching and looking over the brow of a small hill, we saw some fine bucks within fifty yards taking their early meal. They began to sniff the wind and stare about them, when one of us more keen than cautious, or good at taking deadly aim, fired, and off the whole herd scampered; whether either of them was hit we knew not, but the soldier in charge of the dogs, in the excitement of the moment let them go, and a wild chase took place through bog and brake; when, as I galloped on, I observed a man in green coming towards us, and holloaing us to stop; I saw from the line he was taking, he must soon intercept the rest of the party, as he was mounted on an active forest pony, every now and then whistling to call his assistants. Should they come up, our position would be one of great danger; on a moment's reflection, I thought my most prudent plan was to wheel about and charge my enemy in front, leaving the buck to the innkeeper. I was in full uniform and marching order, and the clattering of my sword and the alarming appearance of my charger, coming down full tilt on the little forester, was too much for him, and, notwithstanding the exertions of his rider, he turned and fled by the nearest way to his home.

On the way there happened to be a deep ditch; over it the little pony flew like a bird, leaving his rider in the middle of the water. We then rode to his assistance, helped him out, and used many kind expressions to soothe his ire; but the poor man seemed so astonished with the whole proceeding, he said nothing, only invited us into his cottage to drink some cider. I, half-fearing this might be a ruse to get us into his power and have us up for poaching, began to admire his pony, and offered to give him a good price for it to take with me to Spain as a baggage animal; in the end the bargain was struck and we parted excellent friends, and no questions asked about the shot fired.

On reaching Portsmouth we found a large fleet of transports ready to receive our own and many other detachments; and that evening we embarked the horses, and soon after were on board ourselves. We officers were separated from each other, it being necessary for at least one to be with the men and horses on each vessel. The one in which I was again destined to cross the Bay of Biscay was a fine large, well-found store-ship, with nearly forty horses and dragoons aboard. She was commanded by a young man called Wilson, who was of a higher grade than the usual class of captains of transports in those days; this was fortunate for me, as I was able to treat him partly as a companion. The only other officer on board was a Frenchman, who, having deserted, volunteered his services to the English, and had been rewarded by an Ensigncy in the Chasseurs Britanniques. He was a regular brute, and, on more than one occasion, having shown a disposition to use a large clasp knife, he was not liked by either myself, captain, or crew.[4]

The convoy was a large one, consisting of two or three frigates, several brigs, and smaller ships, making in all a large fleet; now, as the winds were light, towards nightfall the commodore's gun was fired, ordering all headmost ships to shorten sail, and so collect near the men-of-war for protection in the darkness.

The passage seemed likely to be a very long and tedious one, ill-suited to my impatient temper; and I had more than once experienced what a storm was in the Bay of Biscay, I felt very anxious to make the best of our time while we had a smooth sea and steady breeze. Before twenty-four hours of our voyage were over I had ascertained that our captain was an excellent, dare-devil sort of fellow, fond of his bottle and a spree – when opportunity offered – that the mate was a very steady West Country sailor, and that the ship we were in was a first-rate one of her class.

Having made my mind easy on these points, I next day invited the captain to dine with me and drink a glass of some particularly good Madeira, which we had laid in as sea stock. The sea at this time was like a mirror, the ship carrying a lot of sail, making about seven or eight knots an hour, was well ahead and wide of the convoy.

Round went the bottle, evening drew in, the gun fired, and the mate came to announce the signal to shorten sail and drop astern: 'Never mind,' said I, 'take no notice.' Captain Wilson then asked if I should like to run the risk of our being captured by a privateer during the night, for if not he could easily give the fleet the slip; that I told him was exactly what I wished he would do. 'Run on!' was the captain's order, handing at the same time a stiff glass of brandy to the mate. By obeying this order, instead of shortening, more sail was made, so in the morning not a ship of our convoy was in sight. From that night my worthy friend the captain took freely to his glass, and I do believe was never sober; but the mate made good use of his time, and in seven days, after a most delightful voyage, we entered the Tagus.

The mate told me, when he took the pilot on board off the Rock of Lisbon, it was one of the most extraordinary voyages he had ever known, as the sails had only once been trimmed, and the rate of sailing scarcely varied during the whole passage. The remainder of the fleet did not enter the river for some five or six days after us, so I had disembarked men and horses and taken up my quarters in the barracks at Belham before the signal was made, 'A fleet of transports in sight.'

---

4   This unpleasant individual was Ensign Joseph Bernard McDermott, who, notwithstanding his surname, was French and had served in the French Army 1786-1811, including at the Battle of Austerlitz and in the Peninsula from 1808 until his desertion in 1811. He never joined the Chasseurs Britanniques in the field, leaving the Peninsula before the end of the year upon transfer to Dillon's Regiment with which unit he later served at Tarragona. He was promoted to lieutenant in June 1814. In addition to information from Challis, see also Alistair Nichols, *Wellington's Mongrel Regiment: A History of the Chasseurs Britanniques Regiment 1801-1814* (Staplehurst: Spellmount, 2005), p.194.

After a few days, allowed for getting the horses shod and arrangements made for our long march, we started to join the Army, then investing Burgos. The detachment marching to the Army was a large one, consisting of remounts for nearly every dragoon regiment employed. There were two other officers, both most excellent men and thorough soldiers, besides myself of the 12th, and all three of us had been through the country before, both in advance and retreat, and knew well not only the road to be marched, but the difficulties persons, just arrived from England, had to encounter; we also knew, as old campaigners, the best mode of taking care of ourselves where little or nothing was to be had for love or money.[5] When you asked for anything you might require on the march, even in good sized country towns where you knew it could be procured and were willing to pay for it, the invariable reply of the Portuguese would be, 'None here, plenty in Lisbon.' I received the answer myself when two hundred miles from the capital, on asking (from curiosity) for a farthing's-worth of goat's milk at a house at the door of which there were at the moment buckets full.

The inhabitants, at the time of which I speak, were beginning, though slowly, to return to their houses and to collect in the different towns and villages, but their property had been so completely destroyed between the two armies, that there was but little inducement to the richer classes to come back to the miserable remains of their once comfortable dwellings – comfortable to them, but bad at the best in the eyes of an Englishman.

In this unfortunate country – as indeed in all Catholic countries – the priests lead and the flocks follow, and each priest had at the time found his way back to his residence in the villages along our line of march, where it was the parishioners' business to put to rights, or rebuild, his casa before attending to their own; and not only was this done, but all his wants liberally provided for, his larder well supplied, and his cellar well filled.

His house, to look at from the outside, was generally the worst in the place, so as not to attract the attention of the soldier officers passing and searching for quarters; but, to those who knew the secret, it was, from being so well stored within, a most desirable resting-place, especially for a tired and hungry man, so that you will not be surprised to hear that one of us three knowing ones of the 12th always contrived to find himself in the padre's house at the end of a day's march.

---

5   These officers were Lieutenants John Vandeleur and William Henry Dowbiggen. Both, like Hay, had transferred into the 12th Light Dragoons after serving in light infantry regiments. Vandeleur had served with the 71st Highland Light Infantry from September 1810 until wounded at Fuentes de Oñoro; Dowbiggen had come like Hay from the 52nd, and had served with the 1/52nd alongside Hay from March 1811 to March 1812. For Vandeleur's account of their journey through Portugal and into Spain, see Andrew Bamford (ed.) *With Wellington's Outposts: The Peninsular and Waterloo Letters of John Vandeleur* (Barnsley: Frontline, 2015), pp.44-52. In addition to the three officers, a note to the Monthly Return of 25 September 1812 records that the draft for the 12th Light Dragoons comprised the regimental serjeant major, two serjeants, one trumpeter, 33 rank and file, and 94 horses.

At this time the senior officer in command was very strict, as indeed he must be in order to maintain discipline amongst a set of young soldiers. In his own regiment was an officer who, although an older soldier in the service, was junior in the regiment, and from one cause or another a bad feeling existed between them, till at last the latter gentleman found it advisable to withdraw himself from the mess of his brother officers. This he related to me on our march one morning. I said, 'If you are at a loss, come and take your chance with us.' He said he would, and would send his rations; this I told him he might please himself about, but we generally gave our rations to the servants. At this he expressed much surprise, saying no officer, he believed, of his or any of the other regiments, had tasted anything else since they left Lisbon. Now these rations consisted of one pound of coarse meal, musty biscuit, and a pint of sour wine, really not fit to drink.

The padre's, in the place we halted at that day, proved not only a very comfortable one, but well stocked with poultry, hams, sausages, fruit, and very good wine; so, according to our custom, one of my companions established himself as the padre's guest; the other two and friends dropping in at 5 p.m., 'by chance.' I, on this occasion, taking with me my friend Evans (He is now a general officer, a fine soldier, an agreeable companion, and a clever and enlightened member of society).[6] He was quite taken by surprise when he entered the low but clean and neat apartment and found the table spread with a white cloth, all arranged in good style for dinner. 'Ah!' he exclaimed, 'this is a different way of doing things from the Heavys.' Still greater was his astonishment when he saw the various good things put on the table; the priest himself coming in after dinner and ordering some of his best wine to be brought in with him.

Our march the next morning was the stage between Neeza and the pass of Villa Valle – I have before mentioned.[7] I had obtained leave to start before daylight to avoid, as far as possible, the heat of the day, for I was still suffering from attacks of ague and acute pain in my side; my friend Evans, hearing of my intention, proposed to accompany me, and on our way questioned me as to how we managed to keep so good a mess. I answered that if he would promise to keep the secret I would, before the end of the day, initiate him into the mystery of light dragoons' foraging; I took care, however, to say nothing about our proceedings as to getting the priests to provide our good things. Having travelled the horrid road some five or six times I was well acquainted with every turn and corner of it we came to. For at least twelve miles there was not a house or tree to be seen, as we passed through

---

6   This was Lieutenant De Lacy Evans of the 3rd Dragoons, newly transferred to the cavalry after previously serving in the 22nd Foot. After service throughout the remainder of the Peninsular War, latterly on staff employ, he saw further action on the eastern seaboard of America during the closing months of the War of 1812, at Waterloo, in Spain during the First Carlist War of 1835-1837 as commanding officer of the British Legion in the service of Isabella II, and finally in the Crimea where he commanded the Second Division with the rank of lieutenant general.

7   Hay's 'Villa Valle' would seem to be Vila Velha de Rodão, eleven miles north of Nisa.

'View of the pass of the Tagus at Villa Velha into the Alemtejo, by the Allied Army, on the 20th May 1811': Aquatint by Chares Turner after Thomas St Clair. (Anne S.K. Brown Military Collection)

a perfect wilderness of Gumcistus plants, at the end of which was a most precipi-tous and rocky road leading to the river, crossed at that time by a pontoon bridge. From the verge of the hill, before descending to the river, there is a most extensive view of the country on the opposite side, which is truly beautiful and very different from that we had ridden through that morning, green plains, finely wooded with large cork-trees and evergreen oaks – under which I had several times halted to rest for the night – now delighted the eyes of my companion.

What astonished and pleased him most, and myself still more, was the sight of a flock of sheep feeding on the plain. My early start had stolen a march on the farmer to whom they belonged, for the custom of the people was to drive their flocks to feed during the night, to keep them out of sight – not only of the passers by, but the commissariat clerks who were constantly prowling about in search of provi-sions for their divisions, in more distant parts of the country, which were quite exhausted of supplies. On seeing the sheep I said nothing, but pointed to them, making up my mind as we advanced how I could best turn their presence to our account and my amusement.

On the further side of the river between the plain and the long sandy road was on either hand a fringe, if I may so term it, of alder-bushes, and through these were narrow passes only noticeable to those who knew them. By a cunning arrange-ment these openings were so small and crooked as to cause a stranger to suppose the alder-belt to be miles in thickness. Coming to one of the openings I turned my

'General Sir George de Lacy Evans, G.C.B., M.P.' Engraving by George Zobel after Richard Buckner. (Anne S.K. Brown Military Collection)

horse in and told my companion to follow, but keep silent; on getting to the plain side we found the sheep close to us. Now, said I, is our time; you will soon see how *we* contrive to keep so good a table! Draw your sword and charge and select the best.

   In an instant we were amongst the unfortunate sheep, and one fellow's head off his body from the powerful blow of my friend's sharp sword. Just at this moment a tremendous holloaing commenced in our rear; there were the shepherds coming to the rescue. No time was to be lost! The Duke of Wellington's orders were most strict on the subject of anything like bordering on plundering the inhabitants, but, as our prize was not to be relinquished so easily, I was off my horse in an instant and the bleeding carcase was thrown before Evans on his saddle. I cried, follow me! and, mounting again, we dashed into the next small opening across the road at full speed and into the next thicket opposite, in which we had just time to conceal ourselves, when the head of the column made its appearance. The shepherds, getting into the road at the same time, came in contact with the soldiers and stood confounded; then one came forward to speak, and began to address the officer at the head of the party; but he, as well as the others of his regiment, having only arrived in the country a short time, could not understand a word of the language, so, happily for us, the poor shepherds complaints were not comprehended; and no one knew, except my brother officers, that we were in advance.

During this time the state of poor Evans' feelings were beyond description: close to the troops and the commanding officer, with whom he had quarrelled, his dress and saddle stained with blood, and the wretched sheep beside us. However, the Portuguese farmer at last took his departure in despair, and the troops continued their march and poor Evans began to breathe more freely and I to laugh, for which he scolded me most heartily. We continued, nevertheless, to skin a quarter of mutton and pack it in our haversacks on the baggage mules, which shortly came up in the rear of the party.

Very acceptable our morning's prize proved to be at our dinner that evening, when we halted in a miserable, dirty village without even the shadow of a padre's house on which to practise our manoeuvring expedients.

Then we continued our long tedious march towards Salamanca through the exhausted and desolated country. At this town we received orders to halt for a few days to rest the men and horses. I took the opportunity, during my stay here, to ride over the field of battle; although three weeks had passed since the deadly conflict between the two armies, there were still many hundred dead bodies lying unburied – a sad and painful sight even to an accustomed soldier![8]

On leaving Salamanca our large detachment was to break up, and the different parties march by various routes to join their regiments with the Army then investing Burgos. The light dragoons, under the command of Lieutenant Vandeleur, were to proceed by the main road through Valladolid. After a few days march, on our arrival at a town called, I think, Revelo (or Riedo), we found a cavalry depôt under the command of Captain J— of the 3rd Dragoons.[9]

It here became necessary for us to make a minute inspection of our horses, in order that any having sore backs, or that were lame and unserviceable to the regiment, then on active outpost duty, should be left behind. On reporting circumstances and number to the commandant, he insisted that an officer should be left

8   Salamanca having been fought on 22 July, this would imply a date around early August, but the dating of John Vandeleur's letters confirms that Hay has again placed his arrival in the Peninsula rather earlier than was in fact the case. In reality, the party did not reach Salamanca until 7 October, having left Lisbon on 18 September.

9   The location in fact was Arévalo, situated around 55 miles east of Salamanca. The officer in command, whose name either Hay or his editor-daughter chose to disguise for reasons that will become apparent, was Captain John Johnstone of the 3rd Dragoons. See Bamford, *Gallantry and Discipline*, pp.174, 179.

in charge; of course, being senior officer, it fell to my lot, I remonstrated; but in vain. The idea of again going to a depôt was hateful to me; but I could not help myself, and saw, with disgust, the detachment depart the next morning without me.

I think I may have been fourteen or fifteen days doing duty with this horrid depôt of sick and wounded horses, when one morning an orderly dragoon came in, at full tear, to say the English Army had retired from Burgos, that Madrid had been evacuated by our troops; and he brought orders for our depôt to retire on the main road towards the frontier, without loss of time.[10]

Such unexpected and startling news took all parties by surprise; while to myself it caused additional mortification at being cooped up in the rear with a set of disabled men and horses, instead of acting actively in the front with my regiment. Unfortunately, our commandant had not in his composition a particle of what constitutes a soldier; inactive, without energy of mind or body; selfish in the extreme; such was the character of the man, now taken unawares, in charge of some hundred horses, with not above one man to every three. Hence, instead of obeying the order he had received to retire immediately, his baggage had to be got in order, his dinner cooked, and a number of other things done for his personal convenience before the hour of departure was even named; consequently, it was well on into the afternoon before the party, I had to command, were allowed to move. Of this party, some dragoons had as many as five horses to lead; and many of these in such condition as to make it impossible to move at a rate exceeding two miles an hour.

The days were now drawing in, as winter was coming on, so I was not surprised to see the bivouac fires of several of the divisions long before I had completed half the distance to be performed according to the route I had received. I must say, however, I did feel uneasy at observing all those fires ahead of my party, and on my left flank none, except one at a great distance off; and, conceive my consternation, on desiring an active sergeant – the only one I had to depend upon – to endeavour to find out what it meant; and he reported the fires in the rear were the advance of the French, who had already passed through the town we had so recently left; while those on our left were the rear-guard of our troops; those in front, the main body of the English Army!

Therefore virtually my unfortunate party were completely helpless, with nothing between us and the French pickets. Fortunately, the road we were on was a cross country one, and so far we had escaped the notice of both Armies. Of the valiant

---

10 Looking at the dates established by comparison with the Vandeleur narrative, and also at the point at which Hay later re-joined the main body of Wellington's command, this would be around the beginning of November 1812. The orders to pull out of Arévalo were therefore likely not in consequence of the initial withdrawal from Burgos but stemmed rather from Wellington's abandonment of the line of the Duero on 5 November.

Captain J— I saw nothing, he having started off, attended by his lady, to take care of himself, and was now miles away.

I, therefore, had to act, and ordered all horses reported unfit to proceed to be destroyed, and the party to continue to move on all night. By so doing I found by the morning we were out of danger, having regained our proper position in the rear of the infantry. The opportunity I so ardently desired to join my regiment came to me sooner than I expected. A senior officer to myself, Lieutenant Chatterton (afterwards colonel of the 4th Dragoon Guards), who had been on some duty, passing through where my wretched depôt was guard for the night, called on me, as a matter of course, to know what I had there belonging to the 12th.[11] I pointed out several horses now fit to re-join and men recovered, and only required an order from the commanding officer to enable me to march them. The return was made out and taken by him to the colonel; and the next day the good news reached me that the necessary order from headquarters was received, and I was to march with all the men and horses I could select to join – at last – my regiment; an order you may be sure I lost no time in obeying.[12]

I have been so particular, and, I daresay, you will think prosy, in telling so uninteresting a proceeding as my charge of sick men and horses; but my object was to show how unfit selfishness makes men for a post of command, and how often the public and the commander-in-chief of armies are imposed upon by men who have neither principle nor proper feeling, and whose love of self-interest makes their services too often a loss rather than a gain; preventing also the better dispositions of those under them being turned – as they might be – to account. During my campaigns I witnessed many instances of men in high positions for which they were totally unfitted – looking over minor disqualifications – by selfishness alone; this latter fault, to me, has always been indicative not only of a bad officer, but a bad man.

To resume.

On reaching my regiment, how mortified I felt to see the sad change worked on them in the few months I had been absent! On reporting myself, after the long ride before mentioned, from the 52nd to the headquarters of the 12th, I found the men in new uniforms, and the horses and appointments in the best condition. At

---

11   This officer was Lieutenant James Charles Chatterton, whose lieutenancy pre-dated Hay's by one month and who had served in the Peninsula since June 1811. He later commanded the 4th Dragoon Guards, leading them in the parade for Queen Victoria's coronation, and eventually became regimental colonel of the 5th Lancers. Having already been knighted as a KCB, in 1855 he succeeded to the family baronetcy upon the death of his brother and at the time of his death in 1868 was a full general.

12   On a somewhat pedantic note, since he here uses the term colonel as a shorthand for commanding officer, the order for Hay to re-join the regiment could not have come from Lieutenant Colonel Ponsonby as that officer had been wounded in the fighting around Burgos and was himself absent. His temporary replacement, and the man who no doubt authorised Hay's return, was Major the Earl of Waldegrave, who had joined the 12th Light Dragoons in March 1812 to replace the departed Wyndham, but who would himself leave at the conclusion of the Burgos retreat in consequence of his promotion to a lieutenant colonelcy in the 54th Foot.

Right and left-hand views of a Tarleton Helmet of the 12th Light Dragoons.
(9th/12th Royal Lancers Regimental Museum/Richard Tailby)

that time they had but recently arrived from England, and it was a treat to look upon so neat and clean a corps. But what a difference one campaign had made; the men's clothes were actually in rags, some one colour, some another; some in worn-out helmets, some in none; others in forage caps or with handkerchiefs tied round their heads; the horses in a most woeful state, many quite unfit to carry the weight of the rider and his baggage.[13] The edge was indeed off all but the spirit of the dragoons and the blade of his sabre; these continued the same ever, under all privations, willing and ready to work.

The weather had now completely broken, rain fell in torrents, roads knee deep in mud, and the enemy were pressing us hard. Our brigade, commanded by General Anson, formed the rearguard of that part of the Army retiring on Salamanca.[14] It was an open country, well adapted for cavalry, therefore it required the greatest vigilance to check the advance of the French; so on the road by daybreak every

13 Although the uniform of Britain's light dragoon regiments had been altered in 1812 with the introduction of a plainer jacket and with the replacement of the Tarleton helmet by a shako, the 12th Light Dragoons did not receive their 1812 clothing issue until after the conclusion of the year's campaigning. This delay confirms that Hay was quite correct in recalling the men being in helmets, and also explains their ragged state more generally – most likely, the men were still in the uniforms in which they had arrived in the Peninsula eighteen months before. Since Vandeleur reports seeing the new uniforms for the first time that winter, it would seem that the detachment brought out to the Peninsular by that officer, Hay, and Dowbiggen had also not been issued with the revised pattern of clothing before leaving Britain.

14 The 12th Light Dragoons were brigaded with the 11th and 16th Light Dragoons under the command of Major General Sir George Anson.

morning, with horses bridled all night ready for a move if necessary, was the order, and in this manner we reached a place called St. Cristoval, a short distance from Salamanca. Here we remained on outpost duty some days.[15]

It was at this time our belief that it was not the intention of the French commander to pursue the retreating Army further at present, but to content himself with occupying this position on the River Tormes during the winter, which had now begun with rain and bitter cold. Our horses, as I have said, were in a miserable plight from hard duty and bad forage; it was deemed necessary the 12th should be sent into cantonments therefore for a few weeks to recover, taking advantage of the supposed quiet intentions of the enemy. We were relieved by a regiment of German light dragoons, and marched to occupy some villages near Salamanca where the headquarters of the Army then were. Orders were received on our arrival at our new quarters, for foraging parties, under the charge of a subaltern of each troop, to be sent to secure stores; and every precaution taken to secure us the rest of which both men and horses stood in such need.

I happened to be one of the officers thus employed on foraging expeditions, and had proceeded with my party to a village some distance in front where I obtained as much as could be taken back at one time. We were returning with this when a sharp firing began in our rear, and, to my astonishment, I observed the dragoons in our front all in motion, skirmishing and retiring. No time was to be lost; the forage was cast away and our steps bent towards our quarters as quickly as possible; there we found all in confusion. Trumpets sounding 'To horse,' and the troops ready marching to the alarm post. This evening commenced that most disastrous retreat – commonly called 'The Retreat from Burgos.'

The enemy had crossed the river Tormes with a large body of cavalry, and it was necessary for our cavalry to be brought up from all directions, to cover the retreat of the infantry over a large plain several miles in extent, that being the nature of the ground on which began our rear-ward movement. The rain came down in torrents and it was a sad prospect. Our baggage had all been moved off at the first alarm to the rear, and was ordered to take its course towards the frontiers of Portugal. I, like most others, from the orders to retreat coming so unexpectedly, had not furnished myself with any light stock, or even a change of linen, and that night we did not call a halt till long after dark. I had never got rid of my ague, which still continued to attack me regularly every other day, and this was the unfortunate one. I felt myself so ill I could with difficulty keep my seat – wet to the skin and trembling from head to foot.

15 This was the ridge at San Cristóbal, north of Salamanca, where Wellington had hoped to tempt the French to attack him during the early stages of the Salamanca campaign. Just as Marmont had refused to be so drawn, the combined French forces under Joseph Bonaparte and Marshal Soult likewise chose not to attack troops so strongly posted, moving instead to outflank the allied right and thereby forcing Wellington to withdraw south of the Tormes.

On alighting from my horse my batman had a fire made as soon as a few green boughs could be made to ignite; with my feet to that and my head on the root of a tree I laid down, covered by my cloak which was full of water; and this, I conclude, acted like the fashionable 'water-cure,' as, most extraordinary to relate, I never had a return of ague from that day.

Before daylight we were again on our horses, rain still falling incessantly and the roads almost impassable. That night, on getting to the end of our day's march, the famous pig-shooting began, which has often been mentioned in works written on these campaigns. All I can say on the subject is, if ever there was an excuse for men taking whatever came in their way in the shape of eatables, there was a good one on the present occasion. Our regiment for seven days had no rations of one kind or another supplied either to men or horses; for my own part I really must have starved had it not been for the leg of a pig I bought for a dollar from an infantry soldier; this pork, without salt or bread, was all I had tasted during those days, cutting a slice off and toasting it on a long stick by the camp fire. Certainly we had it in our power to eat acorns, which are not unpalatable, not being so bitter as off the oaks in this country.[16]

As our brigade of cavalry covered the retreating columns of infantry in their rear, it was truly one of the most painful and sickening sights I ever before or afterwards witnessed. The roads were strewn with dead and dying men dropped from exhaustion and fatigue; I, one morning, counted thirteen men dead round one fire – I should say starved to death – but whatever opinion I, individually, may have formed, as to the proceedings on the 'Retreat from Burgos,' it would be presumption for me to give; but I fervently hope such another misfortune may never again fall to the lot of a British Army.

Now I shall mention an anecdote which may serve to give one some idea of the state to which the gallant, obedient, well-disciplined soldiers of our Army were reduced by hardship and privation.

The French had pressed us very hard one day, and their cavalry actually made some charges with considerable success between our columns on the line of march. I had been covering the squadron on rear-guard of our brigade, with a line of skirmishers, suddenly I found the French dragoons were disappearing from the front of my extended line and verged to their right. I reported the circumstances, and got orders to recall my party and follow the remainder of the squadron; on my overtaking it, with the rest of the regiment, the column then moved to the rear, near a considerable river.

A short distance to our right, another column of the Army were marching on their line of retreat. On that column the French had concentrated their attention to attack

16   The mass pig-shooting began on 15 November – see Carole Divall, *Wellington's Worst Scrape: The Burgos Campaign 1812* (Barnsley: Pen & Sword, 2012), p.166 – although it does not seem to have been confined purely to that date.

and annoy their advance-guard while fording the river mentioned; consequently, by the time our brigade reached the ford, to which we were directed by the quarter-master-general, a heavy cannonading and firing with small arms was going on.

A division of infantry were formed in close column of regiments on the banks of the river, and crossing in our front, as fast as the nature of the road and the ford would admit, in succession by brigades. About a quarter of a mile off was a considerable town, consisting of, perhaps, five thousand inhabitants. The men of the infantry division, according to custom when halted on the line of march, had piled arms and were allowed to rest or straggle about towards the rear; some went to visit the town, bringing back with them some small trophies in the shape of a loaf of bread or a piece of dry firewood, but sufficient to prove an irresist-ible temptation to their comrades; first ten, then twenty, seemed to move off, of which no notice was taken, but at last the whole lot made a rush at the unfortunate place. To say nothing of the immense danger of an attack from the enemy close in our vicinity, and at that moment actually engaged with some of our troops, and, notwithstanding the exertions of general officers, officers, and non-commissioned officers to recall order, it was not restored till the town was completely ruined. Not only the furniture, but the doors and windows, and rafters of the roofs were broken up, and carried to the camp for firewood.[17]

Such was the undisciplined state of that truly gallant Army in the retreat, in consequence of privations of every kind, which the endurance of man could no longer bear. No provision of any kind was made for them; many had not tasted food for twenty-four hours, and were rendered desperate by the apparent neglect of their superior officers, in not having made any arrangements for the supply of necessaries on the line of retreat; and, I am convinced, that nine-tenths of them would rather have died fighting on the spot of ground on which they stood, than to have had to move further.

I looked on with surprise, and could not help reflecting upon what our tyran-nical General, Crawford [sic], would have done had he been alive and witnessed the scene; at least, to be consistent, he must have hanged half the famished soldiers.

As soon as the division had crossed the river, our brigade, as rear-guard, followed and took up its campaigning ground on a ploughed field; pickets were posted for the night – the squadron to which I belonged being on that duty. Just after the vedettes had been visited and we, expecting a little rest of which we stood in so much need, had stretched ourselves round the watch fire, we were disturbed by the arrival of an order from the regiment directing the squadron to mount imme-diately without sound of trumpet and as little noise as possible, and retire on the brigade which was forming, and wait their arrival. I was ordered at the same time

---

17 Although Hay would seem to be exaggerating the size of the place and the number of soldiers involved, a number of villages were undoubtedly ransacked in this way during the retreat. It is not therefore possible to supply a specific location for this anecdote.

to select thirty men and remain behind to observe the movements of the enemy, either to wait till driven from my post by a superior force, or retire one hour after daylight, if the French did not cross the river.

This move took place about midnight. I fully felt the great responsibility thrown upon me; in fact, the safety of the rear-guard from a surprise from a superior advancing force, also the difficulty of securing a safe retreat for my own small body of men, if necessary to do so, quickly; consequently, I took every precaution in my power to secure both.

When my men had been posted to my satisfaction, and each had explained to him the part he was to act, I took with me a corporal and went to the river-side to patrol its banks, that I might be fully acquainted with the number of fords likely to be passed by the enemy. While on this duty, I thought I observed a white substance showing itself in the middle of the meadow, as the clouds cleared at times and allowed light to shine upon it; going towards it, I observed it move, and, on getting closer, I found a large Spanish wolf-hound taking charge of a young lamb. He kept walking round and round it where it lay, and occasionally lay down himself, to cover it. I was watching this extraordinary sagacity in the poor dog, when my companion, the corporal, dismounted for the purpose of taking the lamb, this the dog would not allow; this movement scared the lamb and away it went, just as the Spaniard, to whom it and the dog belonged, came up; he, after placing the rest of his flock in safety, having returned to look for the lamb. Most *à propos* was this for me, I asked if he knew the road to the place to which I had been ordered to retire. He declared he did not; however, I perfectly knew their practice, on such questions being put to them, so I told him, at all events, he must remain with me. In the first place not thinking it prudent to allow him to tell the French how small our force was, stationed just opposite, within a quarter of a mile of their pickets; and in the next place I felt certain I could, when required, screw some information out of him to guide me on my way.

Daylight came at last, the French drums beat and the troops stood at arms; I took up my place to observe all their movements, and expected every moment to see the columns leave the camps for the different fords; but no, after giving me a good opportunity to observe their strength, and their cavalry had watered their horses, I observed, with no small satisfaction, the whole, after remaining under arms about two hours, disperse to their several bivouacs. I then looked at my watch, and found I had considerably exceeded the time I was ordered to remain after daylight; I repaired to where I had stationed the reserve of my small body, and ordered all the vedettes to fall back by degrees, went up to my Spanish captive and told him to lead the party by the nearest road to Tormes.[18] He could not, he said. I

---

18   There is a confusion of names here: there was a river Tormes, already mentioned, but no town of that name. Assuming that, when Hay later refers to this location as being to the left, he is orientating himself with reference to the line of march towards Ciudad Rodrigo, then most likely he in fact means Tamames.

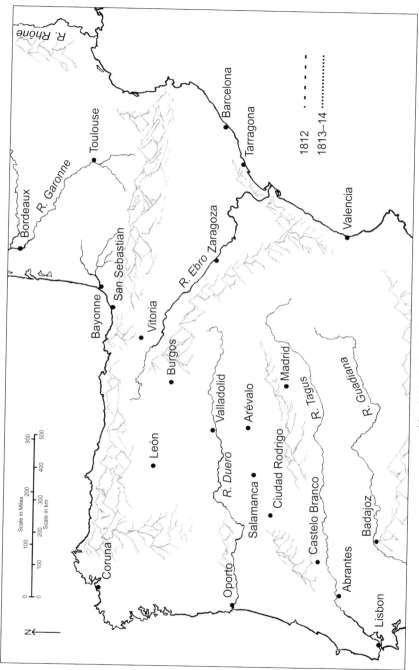

Map 2 Hay in the Peninsula 1812-1814.

ordered a dragoon to move up, take charge of the guide, and load his pistol; at the same time I handed him a dollar and said to him in Spanish: 'If this man attempts to run away, blow his brains out, but if he goes quietly and takes the party by the nearest road, give him this dollar.'

I proceeded without further trouble, but such a sight as here and there presented itself, I pray I might never see again; dying and dead soldiers lying by the dozen on the side of the road, others struggling through the mud, worn out. Round one watch fire were seated about fifty men all of whom declared their perfect incapacity to move a foot further, nor could I induce them to attempt it. I asked my guide if we could in any way avoid these sad sights by taking a more unfrequented path? He was by this time in a better humour, and replied that if I had no objection he would take me through the forest by a narrow way that would only admit of two abreast, but it would save nearly half the distance.

By this path we now took our route, and great was the sensation caused by my party coming right on the head of the advancing column of the brigade, from one of the avenues of the forest in a quarter so unlooked for. At first the general officer in command would not be convinced I had obeyed orders, he had been marching from twelve o'clock the night before and it was by this time about 11 a.m., a distance such as I had performed with my party in two hours with ease; he had not taken the precaution to procure a guide, and, having got into a large forest, had been all night going round and round the same ground, having lost all idea as to where the direct road really was. His excited state of mind from a long night's march and over fatigue made the old gentleman imagine the arrival of our party could mean nothing short of the advance of the enemy's cavalry; and my report, though plain enough, was at first met with considerable doubt on his part, and I was desired, in rather an angry tone: 'As I seemed so well acquainted with roads, to make a patrol on the Tormes road' – which place lay some leagues to our left over the mountains – 'till I met the enemy.'

I selected three of the best mounted dragoons, and set off with great good will on this duty; however, I had not proceeded above a few miles, when the quick and intelligent eye of a thorough and true outpost soldier descried us ascending the steep hillside road from the village in the hollow, and an orderly was despatched to know on what errand I was going, and where. This message came to me from Sir Frederick Ponsonby, who had reached that village some days before, having been sent to the rear in consequence of a wound received before retiring from Burgos. I thought the quickest and most satisfactory way of giving the information he sent for was to go myself and see him. I found him stretched on a form in front of a miserable hovel, with his spyglass in hand, anxiously looking out; for there was no correct information as to where the enemy was, or from what quarter we might expect them.

I was truly delighted to see Colonel Ponsonby, and well knew my report not only would be fully appreciated by him, but how to take advantage of it understood. When I related to him my observation in the early part of the morning, as to the proceedings of the French on the opposite side of the river, his observation immediately was, 'Then it is not their intention to follow us further.' This was my opinion from the first. Colonel Ponsonby's advice in case of difficulty was always received by his superiors with deference, on this occasion he decided at once to recommend the withdrawal of the patrol and the advance of the brigade towards the position destined for them to occupy for the night. After this day we saw no more of the French; their Army halted on the river, and we proceeded towards the frontiers of Portugal.[19]

For six days I had been constantly wet to the skin, never able to change, and living on a small piece of pork and acorns, yet never in my life did I enjoy better health. A few more days brought us to the river Aguida,[20] at which point I commenced to march over the ground, where I had seen some hard fighting and severe duty with that best conducted of all corps, my much respected regiment the 52nd.

I could not help contrasting in my mind the great difference the short space of time (less than eighteen months) had worked on the splendid highly disciplined and well regulated Army that retired before the French, from the position on which we now halted, to fight the battle of Fuentes d'Onore; an Army then in a finer state of equipment or more full of spirit could not have existed. Now all was misery, starved and half-naked, and, worst of all, all discipline seemed at an end. I looked at every place I passed as an old acquaintance, with melancholy feelings, knowing how many of the brave and kind companions of my first days of soldiering had dropped to rise no more, since we had fought together on the banks of the Aguida and Essavera rivers;[21] however, with a soldier such thoughts can be but of short duration, they come like a shadow and are gone.

We now, by long marches, continued our route towards the west of Portugal, which part of the country was selected as our winter quarters. For several days we marched through the miserable and worn out country that had so frequently within the last two years been laid waste by both the French and English armies. Towards the middle of December we reached our destination, and had time to rest ourselves, scattered about in country villages – the largest and best being selected for headquarters.[22]

---

19 The river mentioned here would seem to be the Huebra, which marked the extremity of the serious French pursuit of Wellington's forces on 17 November, which is confirmed by Hay's list of the actions that he was involved in (see Appendix). Since the French, after breaking contact, retired by way of Tamames, this would add weight to the argument for this being the 'Tormes' in the direction of which Hay was sent to reconnoitre.

20 The Agueda.

21 It is unclear which stream is signified by Hay's 'Essavera'.

22 The army was initially held in the rear of Ciudad Rodrigo in case the French renewed their advance, before being dispersed into winter quarters as Hay relates. The 12th Light Dragoons were initially cantoned in the Mondego Valley, before, in the Spring, being shifted further north – first to San Pedro de Sul on the Vouga, and then to Agueda, between Coimbra and Oporto.

The 12th was at this time a pattern family of friends, living with each other on most amicable terms an angry word or look was unknown; and we had the great good fortune to be commanded by one who was not only a most gallant soldier, but most kind and considerate alike to men and officers. His great anxiety at this time was to get his regiment into order, after the long hard work it had gone through, and to do so by giving as little trouble as possible. Troop-watering parade daily was all the military duty we were called upon to perform, all were for a time to rest and amuse themselves.

The men fully appreciated their colonel's kindness and gave no trouble. The village streets, or, rather, roads, in Portugal are at all times bad; but no one who has not lived in the country during the wet season, can picture the state they were now in. The centre of the road from house to house down the long straggling village was like a brook of mud with deep holes, some deep enough to swallow up a mule. The footpaths were of rough stones some three or four feet high; consequently, to move from place to place was not without danger, and required the precaution used by the inhabitants, who carried a stick about seven feet long with an iron spike at the end. Armed with one of these and wearing wooden shoes we amused ourselves visiting each other in our various billets. I had not said anything, on joining them, to my brother officers as to *how* I had managed to live so well on the march from Lisbon to Salamanca; indeed, in the succeeding discomfort I had almost forgotten the priest's house, and only looked forward to my miserable half-pound of ration beef. My servant had, it seemed, a better memory for catering, hence, on my arrival at the village we were to occupy, I was told by the billeting sergeant that my servant had chosen a house in the outskirts, because there was better stabling and plenty of forage. Looking at the horrid state of the road lying between me and my brother officers, I did not much approve of his selection; however, as getting our horses well put up was of the greatest importance, I said nothing and decided to submit to my fate of banishment, and amused myself for some hours by poking about the dirty lanes, hating to enter the houses, which at the best were dirty, close, and evil-smelling. Mine was far from inviting, a long, low, white building, with a broad sort of rough staircase leading to the front door; however, my servant came to me, and asked if he should find out Mr. Dowbiggin and see if he intended to dine with me that day – for we generally lived together. I really did not know if I had anything for dinner, so I expressed a doubt as to whether it would be worth his while to come so far on such a road; he remarked he would ask his servant, and I would find all ready when I chose. On that I went in to reconnoitre and found, to my astonishment, two clean and comfortable rooms opening out of each other. In one was my bed, consisting of a bearskin I carried about with me; and in the other was a table covered with a clean white cloth. Soon Dowbiggin made his appearance – he of all men cared the least about good feeding – came, as I did, expecting only a bit of fresh boiled beef.

We sat down and in came dinner: roast pig, turkey, and other good things; we looked at each other, each suspecting a trick, as a surprise played on the other, said nothing, but partook of what was before us thankfully. When nearly finished, in walked an elderly, corpulent, bald-headed priest, followed by a woman carrying bottles, dried fruits, etc., he hoped we had liked our dinner, and asked if we wanted anything he could supply. The mystery was out! My servant had selected the padre's house which was generally exempted from billets; but not only had he obtained a footing there, but had persuaded the priest that I and my companion were Roman Catholics, thus his great civility and attention was accounted for.

Next morning when the old gentleman knocked at my door informing me the family were assembling to go to mass, my reply explained to him the error into which he had been led, as to my religion; however, the discovery made no apparent difference to him, for, during the time I continued to live in the house, I received the greatest kindness from him; while I endeavoured to give the good old man as little trouble as possible.

One circumstance during my stay took place accidentally that gave rise to some uneasiness. Around three sides of the house facing the garden ran, as is common in many Portuguese houses, a wide verandah where the inhabitants can take exercise in the wet, or lounge during the evenings of the very hot weather. I had generally a visit every morning from some of my brother officers, to take advantage of this verandah to walk about and smoke their cigars. On one of these mornings I perceived, amongst us on the verandah, a stranger – a very tall, stout man – sitting in a stooping position as though anxious not to attract attention. Looking at him carefully I took it into my head that he was not a native of the country; I asked the padre who or what he was, and his reply – that he was a tailor employed by the villagers to repair their clothes at their own houses, a purpose for which he was then there – was given in a manner which rather raised than satisfied my curiosity. I, therefore, went up to the man and addressed him in Portuguese. He replied in the same language, that he did not understand what I said; on which, while he was in the act of stooping his head very low so as to conceal his face, as he pretended to be most interested in his work, I hit him a sharp rap on the back of his head, at the same time telling him, if he could not understand Portuguese, to speak English. The blow and order had the effect desired, and, with an exclamation in Irish, he bounded from his seat and over the verandah, nearly upsetting the old padre in his haste to escape, and causing general consternation. The whole party at once, feeling there must be some unaccountable reason for such a precipitate retreat, joined in pursuit, together with some dragoons who were near the house; away they went across the fields and vineyards, at last the unfortunate tailor was run into, and, on being questioned, it was ascertained that he was an Irishman, who had deserted to the French from a regiment of dragoons the evening before the battle of Talavera.

After joining the French Army he was employed as an officer's servant; but getting tired of his work, he again deserted and allowing his hair to grow very long and all over his face, disguising himself as best he could, he had settled as a working tailor, in the village of Olivenza de Conde, where we found him.[23] I believe he gave the guard the slip on his way to his regiment, the 3rd Dragoons; later he was so unlucky as to be retaken, tried by court-martial, and shot.

My good-natured and kind host was rather put about by my discovery; the man was a Catholic, and had doubtless made himself useful to the priest, to whom his former history was, in all probability, perfectly well-known; he felt somewhat ashamed before me at the idea of being thought to conceal a deserter. His house was at rather an inconvenient distance from the parade-ground, so I, wishing to relieve him of my presence, made that an excuse for leaving, and we parted good friends.

Next, I took up my quarters in the half-ruined house of a Portuguese grandee – a great curiosity in his way. A dandy dressed always, as he conceived, in the pink of fashion, something between the style of his own country and his ideas of English dress. He was, however, one of the best natured men possible and a great fund of amusement to myself and those of my brother officers, who resorted to his verandah and used it as a smoking place and shooting gallery, during the many long wet hours we were forced to spend in the house. On one occasion, using it for the latter, we invited the Señor Hidalgo to join our party. The place from which we shot looked into a sort of old stable-yard, not in the best order. We selected for our mark a door opposite, on which was drawn a white ring with a piece of chalk, at which ring, as a bull's-eye, we fired with ball.

Our host enjoyed the fun and took his turn with the others, but little did he fancy at the time he was committing a murder on his own property. In that small room against the door was kept an enormous pig of some fifty stone weight.

The morning after the shooting-party my host came into my room just as I was going to breakfast, and, with a long face, told me a sad mis-fortune had happened – we had killed his sow which he was fattening for the feast. I, of course, immediately offered to pay for the poor pig, but the señor very wisely observed, 'Why should I pay him for assisting to kill his own pig?' It was for him to pay me, and the payment he offered was the pig for breakfast, which he had brought with him to present.

As forage for the horses became scarce in the neighbourhood, we moved our quarters to other villages; these moves taking place once a month. So passed the winter season of 1812.

Towards spring, new clothing having arrived from England for the men and appointments for the horses, we began once more to look like a dragoon regiment.[24]

23   The location here would seem to be Oliveira do Conde, on the Mondego 35 miles north-east of Coimbra.

24   As noted above, this was the first time that the 12th Light Dragoons received the new pattern of uniforms.

'New Costume of the British Light Dragoons'. Hand-coloured etching by and after Denis Dighton. (Anne S.K. Brown Military Collection)

The Army had been strongly reinforced by several regiments, both cavalry and infantry, and all hands began to get impatient to know whether it was the intention of the French Army to come to visit us in Portugal or if we were to go to them in Spain. It was now the spring of 1813 and some time in the month of April, we got our orders to break up our quarters and commence our march once more to the frontiers.

This time the road was quite new to me. We passed by easy and short stages through a most beautiful and fertile country, which had not been polluted by the presence of the invading Army. We found the inhabitants in all the towns and villages we passed through or where we halted. The monks were in their monasteries, and the nuns in their convents; at both places we frequently rested during this onward march, and always met with the greatest hospitality. No striking incidents took place during this very long but most agreeable march, till we nearly reached the confines of Portugal where we made up to one of the French *corps d'armée*, posted strongly on the opposite banks of the river Esla, not many days' march from the town of Tamora.[25]

---

25   It is to be presumed that the last-named place is actually Zamora. Anson's Brigade, now comprising only the 12th and 16th Light Dragoons, formed part of the Left Wing of Wellington's army on its renewed advance into Spain, being as such under the over-all command of Lt. General Sir Thomas

Before we could move in safety it became necessary to call a halt to enable Lord Wellington to concentrate sufficient force to make preparation to cross the river, to dislodge the enemy from his ground. During the few days we halted for this purpose a large camp was formed which gave me an opportunity to observe, with true gratification, the great change for the better a few months' rest had made on our poor knocked-up and, I may say, undisciplined soldiers of the retreat from Burgos. Every regiment looked brisk and well, and not only had fresh cavalry arrived to join the Army, but fresh and younger general officers to command.

I may here mention an anecdote which, though it did not happen to myself, may be of interest.

The river Esla is, at most times of the year, both rapid and deep; and the bridges in many parts had been destroyed, making it necessary to find fords to enable, at least, the cavalry to cross, for the purpose of reconnoitring the enemy's position. Staff-officers and others had been employed in this way, in the neighbourhood of where we were encamped, for some days without success; when one night the French vedette, on the opposite side of the river, observing that he had a German of the 2nd Light Dragoons as his fellow-watchman, commenced a conversation which ended in an invitation to desert on the part of the Frenchman. The German's reply was, 'How could he dare, not knowing the ford?' On which the other told him to wait till after the patrolling officer had been his rounds, and he would show it to him. When the time came the French soldier, as good as his word, proceeded to the place, at only a short distance from where they stood, and exclaimed: 'Here it is!' The German desired him to pass halfway through first to convince him; this he did. The German thanked him for his courtesy, and each man returned to his post.

When the English officer came round the German soldier informed him of what had occurred, and pointed out the place where was the long-looked-for ford; and by which crossed, soon after daybreak, a strong body of cavalry, by whom the French were dislodged and well beaten.

In a few days after crossing the Esla we again made up to the French rear-guard at a place called Osma where we had a sharp action.[26] The squadron to which I belonged was all the day employed in one of the most irksome and trying duties a dragoon can be exposed to – covering guns. There you have to sit on your horses, inactive, exposed to the fire of artillery, and losing horses and men.

After this we all expected the French would await our arrival at the river Ebro, and dispute our passage of that river. But no; we were allowed to pass unmolested, and came up to the cavalry rear-guard near the town of Valencia.[27]

Graham. The Esla, which runs south to join the Douro west of Zamora, was the first major river barrier faced by Graham's troops and was defended by elements of the *Armée de Portugal*.

26 The action at Osma took place on 18 June 1813, as elements of Graham's column ran into Sarrut's division of the Armée de Portugal: see Smith, *Data Book*, pp.425-426.

27 It would seem that Hay is here remembering things out of sequence. By the time of the skirmish at Osma, the two armies were already over the Ebro. The events here described would have taken place

'British Field Battery and Light Dragoons'. Anonymous ink sketch.
(Anne S.K. Brown Military Collection)

On the high ground above the town we were engaged all one day skirmishing, both parties retiring in the evening, as if tired with the day's work.

Our regiment, officers, men, and horses slept in and about a large church that night. Next morning I was sent by Colonel Ponsonby to make a patrol to the front, to ascertain if the enemy still occupied the same ground as the evening before, when one of those extraordinary delusions of vision, I have often heard of as happening in America, took place.

When I started on my duty about daybreak, the ground was very wet from the rain of the day before; the corn in the plain was very high in the ear – it was June – and over the corn there seemed to hang an impenetrable fog, reaching about as high again as the corn itself. I could not see ten yards before me; consequently, had to feel my way with caution, and may have got about two miles in advance of my regiment – which was halted till I made my report – when I was struck with aston- ishment to observe, as it appeared to me, five French dragoons of enormous size, riding as it were on the top of the corn in the mist. I rubbed my eyes and looked

some days earlier and around the town of Palencia, not Valencia (interestingly, a spelling error also common to Vandeleur's account).

again. I had with me at the time an intelligent corporal and two dragoons. I asked: 'Do you see anything?' pointing in the direction. The answer was by all three: 'Yes, sir, there is a French patrol close to us, seemingly moving on a hill on our front.' My order then was, 'One of you remain on this spot, the others draw swords and let us charge closer to them.' On I went with my two men, but on coming to the place where, as we thought we first saw them, the same objects seemed as far off as ever, and not the least inequality of ground.

We kept following, and the figures receded without our ever getting nearer; thus was I led so great a distance that I halted to reflect what course to pursue, as, for aught I could see, I might be in the middle of the enemy's ranks, when suddenly the morning's sun broke out, dispersing in an instant the fog and the delusion.

At a distance of about a mile in front, could just be seen a patrol of French, retiring, but the pace at which they were going – a walk – and the rapid trot by which I had advanced on them, when I believed them close on me, made their present distance off surprise me greatly.

From my long absence the truly gallant Colonel Ponsonby began to feel anxious, and came on himself following in my track with only his orderly. On arriving at the single man I had left, he was informed of what he had seen, and of my having dashed at the party. That information made the colonel uneasy for my safety; so on he came, bringing with him the man, and came up to me just as I had halted, and was at the moment looking amazed at the party retiring. I related to him what had led me so far on, and pointed out to him the dragoons who could now be seen to have reached the bridge leading into Valencia.

He laughed at me and, in some way I now forget, explained the delusion which he had frequently seen before.

Our party now numbered six; with these the colonel proposed we should now charge down the hill, the plain we were on being high ground, and take our chance of overtaking the French patrol before they were clear of a long causeway at the end of the bridge; however, old birds are not so easily caught. The French dragoons had by this time caught sight of us, and, seeing our intention to come to close quarters, set off at full speed. I pursued them through the streets of the town – the colonel sending back an orderly to direct the regiment to advance and found about two miles further, my friends of the mist had overtaken the rest of their cavalry, which was also in full retreat. I then returned and there ended the morning's work.

(Curious to relate, shortly after I received my appointment in the police, when making my inspection of the men and horses of the 'N' division, I thought I recognised an old acquaintance. I asked his name, and if he and I had not met before. When he replied: 'I did not like to take the liberty of making myself known to you, sir, but I was with you in the 12th Light Dragoons.' He then reminded me of what we saw thirty years before on the plains above Valencia. He was one of the patrol accompanying me on the occasion, his name is Sackes and a brave, steady soldier he was. Since that time he has been superannuated on a good pension from the police fund.[28] He entered the force, when called the Bow Street Patrol, on the recommendation of Colonel Ponsonby.)

After the day of the mist, nothing of moment took place till we drew near Vittoria, where the French, under Joseph himself, stopped to give us battle.

The evening before our brigade halted, about six miles from the enemy on the river Bayas, the Spaniards under General Longa, a guerilla chief, had been sharply engaged during most part of the day.[29]

On our arrival on the encampment ground, I was ordered by Colonel Ponsonby to take with me three men and go and report myself to General Longa, keeping up communications between him and our advance.

On reaching his outposts, I found him still contending with a considerable body of French dragoons, who seemed inclined to force the Spaniards back from the position occupied by them in front of a small village close to the river Zadorra, and I made my presence known to the officer in command.[30]

One of the particular directions I received was not to allow myself to be seen by the French troops if I could avoid doing so. However, the enemy kept advancing and the Spaniards retreating, in the most shameful way, before their cavalry. By-and-by Colonel Elly, quarter-master-general of the cavalry,[31] arrived and did all in his power to rally the Spaniards, and persuade their officers to charge the French on the main road, so as to give the infantry a chance of advancing and taking possession of some stone walls on the outskirts of the village; but all he could say was of no avail, and it appeared very evident that if not checked the Spaniards would be driven back on our pickets. In this moment of great excitement the old colonel

28 Unfortunately, it has not been possible to locate ex-Private Sackes in the pension records of the Metropolitan Police.

29 The Spanish commander was *Coronel* Francisco de Longa. A guerilla leader since 1809, his troops had been incorporated into the Spanish regular army and now formed the Sixth Division of the Spanish Fourth Army. The Bayas flows roughly due north and its valley lay directly across the path of Graham's advancing troops, to which Longa's division was at this time attached. See Oman, *Peninsular War*, Vol. VI, pp.380-383.

30 On 20 July, French forces were thrown out across the Zadorra, which until now had served as the French right flank, to check Graham's advance. These consisted of the infantry division of Sarrut, and the cavalry brigade of Curto, all from Reille's *Armée de Portugal* and under the direct command of that officer. The cavalry under Curto comprised the 22e and 26e Chasseurs à Cheval and the 3e Hussards: see Robert Burnham, *Charging Against Wellington: The French Cavalry in the Peninsular War 1807-1814* (Barnsley: Frontline, 2011) p.82, which corrects the erroneous order of battle given by Oman. Although Oman and Burnham do not agree on the regimental composition of Curto's brigade both agree that it was composed of light cavalry and neither source places any dragoons with the French force, so Hay's memory would seem to be at fault on this point.

31 John Elley had risen from private to lieutenant colonel in the Royal Horse Guards, having enlisted in 1789 and been commissioned five years later. He served throughout the Peninsular War as assistant adjutant general of the cavalry, and served as deputy adjutant general of the cavalry during the Hundred Days. When Hay encountered him, he had recently obtained a brevet promotion to full colonel, and at the time of his death in 1839 was a lieutenant general and a knight.

turned to me, and asked if I would not take command of the Spanish cavalry, rally them, and drive the enemy back. I answered that I had only three men of the 12th with me, but had no objection whatever to join the Spaniards, and try to lead them, if he would give me the orders to do so. His answer was as prompt as my own: 'Then you have the order to do so,' On which I collected some hundred and fifty Spanish dragoons, formed them in the best way I could, and gave them the word of command – to advance – leading the way with my three men of the 12th, both officers and men followed.[32] We dashed in amongst the French, who made a most hasty retreat, and allowed the infantry to rush forward and take possession of the ground that had been lost behind the stone walls.

Nothing but an example was wanting by the Spanish soldiers, who are a brave set of men as need be, and their officers generally as great cowards as live.

By my own rashness I was very nearly being made prisoner, and carried to the rear with the retreating French dragoons. It so happened I was mounted on a very sulky horse in the charge; from his speed I had greatly outstripped both my own men and the Spaniards and had got quite into the middle of the French, then I tried to turn – but no; the horse would not move. Some French, observing me, made a dash to where I was fixed, and, had it not been my own party just then came up, I should have been walked off to Vittoria sooner than I intended. By this time Colonel Ponsonby had come to the front to ascertain what was going on, and, seeing my predicament, most positively forbade me to again ride that horse in front of the enemy; at the same time offering me any horse he himself had to spare.

Next day was the memorable June 21, 1813. Then I saw a truly grand and noble sight, and a most exciting, for any man. But first I must tell you an anecdote, to show you what a fine, noble, unselfish fellow our colonel was.

That morning early, as we were waiting orders to move, he wished me to go with him to the front. We proceeded about five miles in advance, and after reconnoitring the enemy, he said very quietly to me: 'Hay, I am very ill, this is my ague day and I feel it coming on'; leading at the same time into some thick underwood by the roadside. 'I must lie down here till the fit is over; take my orderly with you and keep a sharp look out, and if, from any movement of the enemy, we are to have anything to do, send me word immediately; but do not tell any one I am unwell.' It may have been about 10 a.m. when the regiment came from the camping ground to where I was waiting the recovery of my colonel; and he had to resume his work. We were then formed into a brigade consisting of the 11th, 12th, and

---

32   There were no dragoons attached to Longa's force; his only cavalry unit was the Húsares de Iberia which had originally formed the mounted element of the Guerrilla band led by 'El Medico'. Their officers, at least, wore conventional hussar uniforms by this stage of the war, so it is unclear why Hay calls them dragoons (although note that he does the same with reference to French light cavalry too, so the term may be intended to be understood in a more generic sense). See René Chartrand, *Spanish Army of the Napoleonic Wars (2) 1808-1812* (Oxford: Osprey, 1999) p.33.

16th Light Dragoons.[33] As we proceeded on our march over some rather rough uneven ground, keeping within sight of the river Zadorra – which is a deep, sluggish stream, with broken banks and not a ford anywhere – we could plainly see the divisions under General Hill, which formed our extreme right, commencing their operations.[34]

I must, in speaking of the battle of Vittoria, deviate, in a small degree, from my purpose of writing only an account of my personal proceedings, and give a short description of the day's work in which so many of my fellow soldiers were actively engaged, for this reason.

In all former battles or affairs in which I had the honour to be engaged, no opportunity was afforded me of looking on for any time inactively; and in my opinion it is the greatest presumption for any subaltern, who has the slightest pretence to say he has done his duty, to offer to the public a description of a battle in which he has taken part. If indeed a battle is to be described, it can only be done by those staff-officers immediately employed by the commander-in-chief to reconnoitre the ground for the position, and who, during the battle, have sufficient leisure to observe the movements of the different divisions or corps destined to occupy the ground, with which they are already acquainted.

For my own part, I have been in my share of engagements and feel certain that my time and attention were fully occupied by the movements of my own regiment and those troops near and connected with it. But the battle of Vittoria was an exception as, from the nature of the ground allotted our brigade to move over and take up our position, we were enabled to see for miles, while we ourselves were unable to take part in whatever was going on.

From our route Vittoria seemed to stand like a large town in the midst of an even plain with high wooded hills, or mountains, in the background; but that in reality is not the case, as before reaching the plain from where we were posted, there lies (unobserved by us) a space of ground broken by deep wooded ravines.

We were from time to time the mark for a salvo of artillery; but the attention of the batteries was directed principally against the moving columns of infantry, either contending for the passage of the river, or directed to clear the ravines of the French troops in possession; hence we were not much molested and had fair time for observation. Nothing could exceed the magnificent sight or the excitement with which one viewed the progress of our gallant men.

We saw distinctly the troops, on the hills above the town, hotly engaged disputing every inch of ground as the enemy gradually gave way; on our left

33 Hay is here in error: the 11th Light Dragoons was one of the regiments sent home from the Peninsula at the close of the 1812 campaign, although they had been brigaded with the 12th and 16th prior to that point and would be so brigaded again during the Waterloo campaign.
34 Hill, with the 2nd and Portuguese Divisions and the Spanish division of Morillo, opened the allied attack by assaulting the Heights of La Puebla on the left of the French position: this was intended to focus attention away from the main attacks against the French centre and right.

flank we heard the constant roar of artillery, mingled with small arms, where Sir Thomas [Graham] was attacking and driving the French over the high broken ground, where infantry only could act.

Close to our front were the troops contending for the bridge over the Zadorra, leading by the main road to Vittoria. Thus, watching others and ourselves moving very slowly, the forenoon was passed.

Towards afternoon it seemed, from where we stood, as if the whole forces we had seen fighting at a distance had got close together and were contending hand to hand. Still the firing on our left continued till about 6 p.m., it was succeeded by a cheer from our troops, the bridge was carried, and a free passage opened for our brigade and the horse artillery.[35]

To this point we directed our march, crossed the bridge, and formed on the opposite bank in brigade of squadrons: the one to which I was attached was in the rear of all, in fact I commanded the left half squadron of nine squadrons moving right in front.[36]

In this order we advanced, first at a trot then at a canter, and soon came in sight of the French cavalry. On seeing our advance, advantage was taken of some broken ground at the extreme end of the plain over which we were advancing towards them, to halt and form for our reception.

As we drew closer this appeared madness, as their numbers did not exceed half ours. Our trumpet sounded 'The Charge,' when, on coming up to what seemed a regiment of dragoons awaiting their doom, their flanks were thrown back and there stood, formed in squares, about three thousand infantry. These opened such a close and well directed fire on our advance squadrons, that not only were we brought to a standstill, but the ranks were broken and the leading squadrons went about, and order was not restored till a troop of horse artillery arrived on our flank and, within about a hundred yards, opened such a fire of grape shot on the French infantry, that at the first round I saw the men fall like a pack of cards. That was sufficient and off they went, and our regiments were reformed. Night was now setting in and we went no further.[37]

So ended the battle of June 21, 1813. Certainly the very grandest sight I had as yet seen in my travels as a soldier.

The nature of the ground and the fine day gave it truly the appearance of one of those pictures of a battle drawn from fancy.

---

35   Hay is here referring to the bitter fighting around the village of Gamarra Mayor which, along with its bridge across the Zadorra, was eventually captured by the infantry of the Fifth Division.

36   Hay's account of nine squadrons corresponds to his earlier error of stating that the 11th Light Dragoons were still part of the brigade; there were in fact only six squadrons in Anson's two regiments at this time.

37   Vandeleur, by contrast, suggests that the French were charged more than once: see Bamford (ed.), *With Wellington's Outposts*, p.93.

Our brigade bivouacked for the night nearly on the ground on which we were brought up by the French squares. It took some little time next morning to get things in order for our moving, and it was there a sergeant's party brought into our headquarters a small military chest of dollars they had hit on while on night duty; most justly, the general-in-command took upon himself to distribute the prize among the officers and men according to their rank in the service, I recollect my share came to thirty-three dollars.

Finding I had time on hand, I thought I might take a ride over the field of battle, so started towards the town of Vittoria, and certainly I saw a sight which astonished me. I was well prepared, from having on a former occasion gone over the fields of hard contested fights, to see heaps of dead and dying, but I was not prepared for the number of guns, gun-carriages, ammunition-waggons, carriages – some of them actually still containing ladies – baggage of every description, horses, and mules literally covering the ground. I hated the idea of plundering; consequently, did not appropriate to myself any single thing, though I am sure I might have done so with impunity as several others were doing, I was satisfied to look with surprise at what had been achieved by our victory.

It appeared to me to be the most total over-throw of the grand Army of France, that could well be imagined. While I was standing contemplating the scene around me, a Portuguese soldier came up laden with plunder and dragging a very fine mule, he had taken from one of the guns. I offered him the dollars I had received for it, which he gladly accepted. I led the animal back to our camp and gave him into the charge of my servants. I am particular in mentioning this circumstance about the mule, as I shall afterwards relate a curious story concerning him.

Towards afternoon we followed up the march of the retiring French Army, next day we came up to their rear-guard, and, I must say, I was surprised to see anything like an Army, after the sight of complete overthrow I had witnessed the day before.

However, there they were, and, as the ground was in their favour, we did not provoke them to fight; nevertheless, I thought at the time I could, with a brigade of cavalry, have made two strong columns I came across when on patrol, lay down their arms; but it was not then, nor is it now, my business to say why that was not done.

That evening we marched through Tolosa, and took up our quarters in some straggling hamlets a few miles out of the town. Some days later we advanced again to assist in reconnoitring San Sebastian; and, finally, put up at a town called Ernani, in which place the 12th remained till the arrival of Sir Thomas Graham, to make it his headquarters during the operations going on at San Sebastian, when the regiment was ordered to occupy some mountain villages about twenty miles in the rear.[38] I was ordered to remain at Ernani with a small party of dragoons, to

---

38   The location is in fact Hernani, five miles south of San Sebastián.

act as orderly officer to Sir T. Graham and keep up his communication with other parts of the Army: on that duty I was employed some weeks.

When I received orders to re-join I found my regiment quartered in villages quite among the hills which were wild and, to me, delightful to behold.

Now I had always been a sportsman, and amongst my other occupations had not missed the chance of picking up, when he came in my way, a good-looking greyhound, and by this time I had collected at least six or eight large, rough, handsome dogs. The people in the villages were simple and unsophisticated, knowing and having seen little beyond the flocks of sheep and goats they tended, and which comprised their means of existence and sole employment. There, the morning after my arrival, seeing the hills covered with grass and fern so inviting and so like a place where, in my own country, I should have expected to find hares, I started with my greyhounds, as soon as it was light, intending to amuse myself with a course. I had gone some distance, quite out of sight of houses, my attention wholly taken up in beating about the side of a sort of glen, when suddenly I heard the most dreadful shrieks, and cries of fear, and driving of sheep in all directions.

I thought it could be nothing less than that the French had driven our people back and reached the villages. To call my pack together, and proceed in the same direction, was the work of a moment; but the nearer I came to the rear of the flying shepherds and children the more furious were their yells. I saw coming towards me some men, armed with guns and long sticks, holloaing out 'The Wolves!' It turned out on explanation, that those who first saw my grey-hounds mistook them for wolves, and were consequently frightened out of their life – a feeling shared by their sheep, which they drove to the villages for safety. I enjoyed the joke and so, poor things, did they.

Talking of this alarm reminds me of another at the battle of Vittoria when on our advance, we had arrived at our quarters rather earlier than usual.

Some days previously there had been reports that we were getting into the near neighbourhood of the French, though we had not seen them ourselves. We took the advance posts, where the country admitted, in regiments in turn, making the duty lighter. This day, the village the 12th were to occupy may have been distant from the other regiments some six or seven miles. The country was flat, but with occasional heights from which a considerable extent could be seen. Colonel Ponsonby, always anxious to spare his men from fatigue, and himself never, had not only with his intelligent eyes, made a perfect recognisance of the country, but had directed officers to do the same, and report to him all to be seen or heard within a certain distance – perhaps twenty miles. These observations all confirmed in his own mind the idea there was nothing to be apprehended from the enemy during the night, at all events. Consequently, small outposts parties, consisting of non-commissioned officers, were placed at short distances from our front.

The remainder of the regiment were allowed an indulgence which had not been enjoyed for several weeks, i.e., to wash, and dress, and to unsaddle their horses.

We had at this time a very excellent commissary and a great favourite with every one, a Mr. M—.[39] He moved about as a commissary had a right to do, with many more comforts than would have been consistent with the equipage of a fighting officer, and amongst others a wife.

M—. took every opportunity of showing kindness to the officers for whom he officially provided, and, whenever the quarters admitted, would give them a good dinner at his own casa. That day he was well put up and we were for once all together, he, therefore, asked the entire party – consisting of about twenty – to dine.

We assembled and did ample justice to the good cheer provided, and were enjoying ourselves sipping some of the best Douro and smoking cigars, when suddenly the door of the room burst open, and in rushed the commissary-general's wife, and dropped in a fainting fit; after her came two or three servants only able from fright to utter the words 'The French,' Questioning a clerk, who came in as well, he said the French dragoons were in the streets cutting down all who came in their way.

What to do it was difficult to say, for the front door was besieged with frightened persons coming for protection; the wall way was one mass of men, women, and children, intermixed with mounted muleteers and dismounted, running dragoons with their saddles to where their horses were stabled or tied up.

The month was June; the heat was excessive, of course the roads were very dusty, so nothing could be seen distinctly through the clouds raised by the confused and screaming crowd. No exit could be made at the back as it was surrounded by a high wall, so into the crush it was necessary to throw oneself, and struggle through as best able till reaching his own quarters, where he had left his horse and servant.

Meanwhile, the most active of the dragoons had mounted, and were galloping to the alarm posts (a place appointed for assembly when near an enemy).

On reaching my stable I found my charger nearly ready and, mounting, I started for the meeting place, surprised to encounter no French cavalry, and still more so to see many of our own troops had arrived, and were arriving, from all directions. The colonel, having collected as many men as he could in the first confusion, had gone to the front, from whence the enemy were said to be coming. There he found our outpost parties quite ignorant of alarm, having seen no one.

On more strict enquiry it proved that some muleteers had seen in the distance a squad or two of Spanish guerillas passing at a trot on some expedition of their own, and had mistaken them for the French, flying in terror to the village where

---

39 The commissary attached to the 12th Light Dragoons at this time was Deputy Assistant Commissary General William Myler; he had been in the Peninsula since March 1812, but between May and December of that year he was serving elsewhere and only returned to the 12th when his replacement was dismissed as incompetent. Sadly, he was to die – apparently of illness – in January 1814.

we were, raising the alarm as they came. It did not end with our regiment, as many had fled even to the headquarters of the brigade, six miles off; one of the fugitives reported the French had attacked the village and cut the 12th to pieces, he – the valiant bearer of the report being the only person who had escaped.

When all the patrols had returned and made their report that there was no enemy in sight, the regiment was dismissed, and we returned to the commissary's to talk and laugh over the ridiculous occurrence.

We found, however, our host, who was usually a light-hearted man, and well able to see a joke, could not be roused from the state of stupor into which he seemed to have fallen, At last the reason was apparent: his wife and faithful servant, Jose, with all the money they had collected, were missing! On learning this we naturally felt much for poor M—, and our kind-hearted colonel at once took steps to arrest, if possible, the supposed fugitives.

Parties were started to overtake them, if on the route back to Portugal, and to search in all directions for their place of concealment; but as each party returned reporting no trace could be found, it was about to be given up as hopeless, when one of the muleteers remarked: 'He had better return to the position taken up by Jose, and tell him the danger was over.' The commissary was thunderstruck at this speech, and was told in explanation, that his poor faithful servant had thought of saving his master's property as far as lay in his power, so had hurriedly placed the boxes containing the doubloons on one of the mules, Mrs. M— and himself on another, and with the mule-conductor, gone off to the neighbouring forest; and first helping the lady up into a thick tree and himself ascending another, the conductor handed up the money-boxes which he lashed to the branches, hoping to remain in safety till the storm passed by. Sure enough this was found to be the case, and the poor things were brought back, more dead than alive from fright, to the no small delight of poor M— and of us all. The Portuguese were, and had reason to be, very much afraid of falling into the hands of the French.

(In my opinion, from experience, a false alarm is ten times more trying to the courage of a soldier that any battle that could be fought. I was also witness to another, which took place in the middle of the night after a long and fatiguing march, when driven by the enemy across the Coa. I was at that time in the 52nd. The country was very rugged and covered with wood, and the men had only reached the encamping ground at dark, nearly worn out with fatigue. Arms were piled, and the men lay down beside them to rest, when some bullocks, that had broken away from their drovers, came at full gallop over the sleeping soldiers, knocking down the piled arms; the greatest confusion and dismay ensued, for many were doubtless dreaming of the French cavalry who had pursued them all day, and woke to find their dreams apparently realised!)

But to resume. After remaining in the mountain villages a few weeks, we again moved, indeed we never remained long in one place; wherever the enemy showed a disposition to attack was the place for the light cavalry to be near. In this way we went on till the siege of San Sebastian. Shortly after we crossed the Biddasoa, and so into the French territory for the first time.[40]

The Army were now actively engaged dislodging the French from a line of forts which were very strong. During this business we again had that most unpleasant of all duties – covering guns. We were whole days together under the enemy's fire, I recollect one day in particular: Colonel Ponsonby had gone off on some excursion nearer the scene of action where the infantry were engaged, and had left Colonel Bridger, a good old man in his way, but not an active soldier, in command of his regiment.[41]

We were placed behind some small hillocks out of sight of the enemy's forts, to cover Captain Ramsay's battery of horse artillery which was firing at them.[42]

The shot and shell from the forts generally struck the high ground, recoiled, and came down among our horses. Colonel Bridger kept shifting his ground, and at last took up his position behind a great willow-tree. Now, I must confess, that I and other young and thoughtless fellows were wishful of disturbing the old fellow in a very unkind way.

At the top of the hill, just in range of the French forts and the willow, was a dry ditch, which we got into, one of the party keeping a look out with a spyglass, and the rest got on to the top facing of the ditch; when the one with the glass saw the fuse put to the gun, he gave the word 'Down,' we jumped into the ditch safe enough, but the shot struck the top of the hill in line with the tree under which the colonel sat and then went right through the branches. This foolish amusement we continued till his resting-place became quite unsafe: and the colonel, finding out the cause, an order was of course given us to desist.

However, by this time the French had got so good a range of our post that we nearly suffered ourselves, in a way we justly deserved.

On being ordered to retire from the ditch, the colonel invited us to partake of something to eat and drink – certainly as good a pastime – and a large piece of boiled salt beef was provided, round which about eight officers were seated on the ground, when one of the shots we had been provoking from the battery, came right into the midst of us, knocking the beef and plates about our ears, rebounded and took off the arm of an orderly, who was in the act of putting a nosebag on his horse, and killed the animal. We were sitting close together, and it was quite a miracle

40   Wellington's troops forced the line of the Bidasoa on 7 October 1813: see Smith, *Data Book*, pp.459-460.

41   As well as getting his rank wrong, it is odd that Hay here refers to the regiment's new second-in-command, Major James Bridger, as old, for he was only 34 at this time. Bridger had got his majority when Waldegrave left the regiment in December 1812, having previously commanded its depot as a senior captain.

42   This was I Troop, Royal Horse Artillery, commanded by 2nd Captain William Norman Ramsay of Fuentes de Oñoro fame, which on this occasion was deployed to support the troops of the Spanish Fourth Army. See Nick Lipscombe, *Wellington's Guns: The Untold Story of Wellington and his Artillery in the Peninsula and at Waterloo* (Oxford: Osprey, 2013), p.333.

some of the party were not killed; but it is an old and true saying, 'Every bullet bears its billet.'

For several days we remained at this work. The Army, after dislodging the French from their strong positions, advanced their headquarters to the town of St. Jean de Luz; and our cavalry brigade took the outpost duty near a village called Vientes.[43]

Although we had now fairly established ourselves in the Basque Province of France, we had not improved our condition either as regards quarters or forage for our horses. Winter had set in, and very severely too, we were nearly starved to death with cold; and our nags were only kept alive by eating chopped whins.[44] Still we had very hard duties to perform – constant fighting going on for days.

The villages were looked upon as a sort of neutral ground, and there was a kind of tacit understanding between the French and ourselves not to interfere with each other when getting forage there. They generally went first, and after helping themselves, rang the church bell, as a sign we might come on.

So far things went smoothly enough, but after a time a movement was made in the night to drive the left wing of the French Army across the Nivelle, and this engagement, in which they were so completely worsted, perhaps had the effect of putting them out of humour, and rendering them extra suspicious of our movements; anyhow soon after the action of the Nivelle, the following contretemps occurred.[45]

On the verge of the extreme outpost, at the top of a considerable hill, stood a white house, which we had named the Major's House of Vientes.[46]

At this house, on our return to cantonments, Colonel Ponsonby took up his quarters, he having been entrusted with the responsible and arduous duty of the charge of pickets, who also occupied part of the house and outbuildings as their headquarters.

The squadron picket may have been a mile further on the road to St. Jean, and at the white house was a subaltern's detachment under the immediate supervision of Colonel Ponsonby, either for patrol duties or others as he might deem fit.

Leading up to the house from the main road from St. Jean to Bayonne was a long straight avenue; about a mile and a half along this road from the avenue gate were posted our two advance vedettes; while at the top of the hill, and nearer the entrance to the avenue was a single vedette as a line of communication; and at the head of the avenue, near the house, was posted a dismounted dragoon, on look out.

---

43   Unknown location, presumably now absorbed by the sprawl of Biarritz in intervening years.

44   Whins: an archaic term for gorse.

45   The Battle of the Nivelle took place on 10 November 1813: see Smith, *Data Book*, pp.476-478.

46   If it is assumed that 'major's' is a typographical error and that 'mayor's' is meant, this was the Château de Barrouillet, commonly referred to as the mayor's house in many contemporary accounts as it belonged to the mayor of Biarritz. The site is today the location of the Biarritz toll-booth on the A63 autoroute: see Ian C. Robertson, *Wellington Invades France: The Final Phase of the Peninsular War* (London: Greenhill, 2003) p.168.

On the occasion I speak of I was officer on this picket. Now, when on so important a duty, as an outlying picket, we never – at least I can speak for myself – took off a particle of clothes. Patrols took place every hour during the night, consisting of a non-commissioned officer and men, and by the officer or Colonel Ponsonby himself, the last thing at night and a little before day-dawn; horses were kept bridled ready to mount at a moment's notice.

The colonel had made his rounds in one direction, and I had made mine in another, we found all quiet, and returned. He, being tired, said he would lie down for a few minutes, and I might order the picket to unbridle and feed their horses. This order was given, and I was taking a stroll in the avenue, when, to my utter horror and amazement, I saw enter at the other end what seemed to me in the mist of morning a host of French officers and dragoons preceded by a trumpeter.

I was almost paralysed; I called to the soldier behind to turn out the picket; sent the first man to call the colonel; then rushed down the avenue, with the first men who had mounted, to meet, as I supposed, the advance-guard of the French column, which, having shot our vedettes, were now coming to surprise our pickets.

Instead, however, I was met by a trumpeter, sounding a parley, and an officer with a white flag; bad as this was, their having got beyond our outposts, it was a relief. I halted the party, drew my men across the road, and waited the arrival of Colonel Ponsonby; then an explanation took place.

It was an *aide-de-camp* of General Reynier's, but with a much larger retinue than was customary, or than such an occasion required. Our colonel would not listen to a word he had to say till he retreated to neutral ground.[47]

Unfortunately, however, the French officer had been sufficiently far into our lines to observe a large body of foragers ready to debouch into the village, when the church bell announced the retreat of the French. Not understanding the meaning of the men being drawn up, he reported on his return what he had seen to his general who, from the previous week's attacks, expected we intended several more of the same kind; therefore, when the foragers were put in motion, and began to show themselves, the French drums beat 'To Arms,' and in less than a quarter of an hour, instead of quietly taking our breakfast at the Major's House, we were hotly engaged, and the squadron in which I was, not only lost many men and horses, but we were nearly cut off bodily, while covering the retreat of the foragers, many of whom were taken prisoners.

With these sort of things going on to amuse us we passed a dreary uncomfortable winter; and so ended the year 1813.

---

47   The French officer could hardly have been an aide of Reynier, who had not served in the Peninsula since 1811 and was at this time a prisoner of war following his capture at Leipzig. Most likely the officer was an aide to Général de Brigade Jean-Pierre-Antoine Rey, a brigadier in Soult's *Armée d'Espagne* (not to be confused with Louis Emmanuel Rey, who had been governor of San Sebastian).

'The Mayor of Bordeaux, raising the white cockade on the appearance of the British' Engraving
after unknown artist. (Anne S.K. Brown Military Collection)

Towards the beginning of 1814, we advanced to Bayonne, and crossed the river
Adour, the cavalry by swimming horses, and the infantry by a bridge of boats; we
had now established ourselves in rather a better country, where the houses, though
in many instances deserted by the in habitants, were more comfortable and the
natives more civilised than the Basque peasants.[48]

Our quarters for some days were in the immediate neighbourhood of a considerable town, Dax. There we had made up our minds we would be left in peace, at
least for a time, as the weather was very severe and the country deeply covered
with snow. But there is no rest for the wicked. One morning in the midst of a heavy
snow-storm a sudden and unexpected order came from headquarters for the 12th
to march immediately, and attach themselves to the 7th and other divisions then
on their route, by another road to Bordeaux.[49]

48   The Adour crossing began on the night of 21-22 February 1814, with a squadron of the 12th crossing
     the following day – swimming the horses as the famous bridge of boats was not yet complete – as one of
     the first reinforcements of the initial bridgehead. See Bamford, *Gallantry and Discipline*, p.221.
49   Bordeaux was entered on 12 March by a corps under Sir William Beresford, composed of the infantry
     of the Fourth and Seventh Divisions, the hussars of Vivian's Brigade, and two squadrons of the 12th

Although we had a wild and uncultivated country to pass through in winter, our comforts were great in comparison to what I had endured often since leaving England.

We had now got into a part of the country not in the least attached to the Bonaparte dynasty, therefore we were all welcomed on our arrival at the end of a day's march by the host of a comfortable inn, well provided with beds and good board; while our poor half-starved cattle had good stabling and plenty to eat.[50]

After a long march we reached Bordeaux, in which town, I honestly confess, I spent the happiest days I had ever known then or since.

At first starting a singular adventure befell me. I never gave myself much concern about what sort of house I was to be put up in, provided my servant reported favourably of the stabling accommodation. I had been told where my billet was but did not trouble to go and look at it, so to pass the time, while the baggage was being unpacked and my room put to rights, I looked into the quarters of my captain, whom I found seated with the family of the house. I was introduced and took my seat with the rest, when a gentleman, who seemed to have come into the room out of curiosity to see the English officers, came up to me, and after a few civilities, enquired where I was quartered, I told him, and he said: 'That house will never do, the landlord has left it, and you will be most uncomfortable.' I assured him quite the contrary, and that I did not require anything of the landlord. He then invited me to accept quarters in his house which was close at hand.

I begged to be excused; but all I could say was of no avail against my afterwards kindest of friends; the more I refused the more determinedly did he persist, and my captain also recommending me to accept the offer, with some reluctance I consented to do so. He at once took my billet, had it changed, and I became the guest of M. Plantagene, and his kindness to me exceeded what one could believe possible in the best of landlords.

He not only gave up to me a suite of elegantly furnished apartments for my use, but insisted on my becoming his guest and visitor, requesting that I should, moreover, invite every day as many of my brother officers as I wished to dine at his table.

He sent his medical man to attend to my health; his tailor to make my clothes; and his bootmaker to receive my orders. He led me through his house to where his own chest containing his money was deposited, and, opening it, told me there was still, notwithstanding the war, enough money to meet my expenses as well as his own. In truth, unremitting attention to my wants made me feel quite uncomfortable, though filled with sincere gratitude. M. Plantagene spoke English perfectly, and was married to a very pretty, amiable American woman.

Light Dragoons (the third squadron remaining around Bayonne for the time being). See Bamford, *Gallantry and Discipline*, pp.222-223.

50 'Cattle' is used here in the archaic sense of 'beasts' – Hay is talking about the regiment's horses.

Not only to myself, but to all of us, it was something new to be in such good quarters as those we now occupied and of which the French, by crossing the Garonne, had left us in quiet possession.

One squadron, however, was sent across the river to reconnoitre the enemy's position, etc. When on this duty one morning early, I had got a considerable distance from headquarters, and into a thickly wooded bank of the river Dordogne, from there I observed – myself unseen – the movements of a party of French soldiers, seemingly very busy moving a piece of artillery. I continued to observe their movements and found their intention was to plant the gun, masked by branches and straw, built up as a stack, so as to command a complete range of the road leading from the side I was on, down to a ford that crossed the river to their side. The gun was then loaded, and all retired except one man, who, to all appearance, was only doing sentry duty. All this excited my curiosity and astonishment, for in the length of time I had been, both as a cavalry and infantry soldier, close to the French on outpost duty, I had never seen the least design to take unfair advantage of patrols or pickets. On the contrary there was an understanding between the outposts of both Armies, that made you feel you were dealing with true and honourable soldiers, above taking petty advantages for the mere destruction of the life of an individual employed on a similar duty.

I therefore stole away, unseen from the opposite side, leaving a dragoon to watch, and came by a circuitous route into a road leading back to the village.

I puzzled myself a great deal as to how best to give information of what I had witnessed, when, most opportunely, I met the curé of a neighbouring parish (these men were all in favour of the Bourbon dynasty, therefore, inclined not only to be civil to us, but when not afraid of being discovered gave us information), I entered into conversation and learned he had heard it was the intention of His Royal Highness the Duke d'Angouleme to be in that neighbourhood that day; and he believed he purposed passing down the very road I had observed as well covered by the gun from the enemy. It immediately occurred to me that the information had been conveyed by a spy in the secret of His Royal Highness's movements, and preparations had been made by them accordingly.[51]

To frustrate their design now became my object; I, therefore, directed my remaining dragoon to take one direction while I took another to look out for the royal party. The man I sent soon returned, and reported that the duke with his staff and two orderlies of the staff-corps were riding in a direction for the road leading to the ford with a view, no doubt, of reconnoitring the French troops on

51 Louis Antoine, duc d'Angoulême, eldest son of the Comte d'Artois, had arrived in southern France in response to the Bordelais recognition of his uncle as Louis XVIII. In that Britain had not yet backed this claim, this caused some political difficulties for Wellington, for which see Oman, *Peninsular War*, Vol. VII, pp.388-399. It is impossible to independently verify the plot against him that Hay outlines here.

'S.A.R. Monseigneur le Duc d'Angoulême, Grand Amiral de France' Hand-coloured
stipple engraving after unknown artist. (Anne S.K. Brown Military Collection)

the other side. I at once put my horse to the gallop, and came up with them in time
to arrest their further progress towards the point of danger.

I addressed myself to the Count de Dumas et Gramont, who repeated my information to His Royal Highness;[52] he had been so completely deceived by those who
had wished to lead him into this trap that he seemed to think I had made a mistake
in my observations, and said the few French, who guarded the other side were all

---

52 Presumably Héraclius de Gramont, duc de Guiche and later 9th duc de Gramont in succession to his
    father, who was then serving as an aide to Angoulême.

favourable to his cause. I, therefore, wishing to prove myself in the right, begged he would allow me to show him how much I suspected he had been misled by his informers.

He halted. I then, unobserved by him, brought forward my own man and his two orderlies at a trot, in sight of the sentry on the hill, who, evidently in a state of great excitement, judging from his aim, fired the masked gun, letting drive a shower of grape shot at me and my men, but which fell harmless behind our horses. I then withdrew and went back to where I had left the duke, smiled, and pointed to the place. I soon afterwards became acquainted with His Royal Highness, who never forgot the adventure; and, during his and my stay at Bordeaux, I received marked attention from him, he frequently sending me an invitation to his dinner-parties.

Our tour of duty as an outlying squadron having ended, we again returned to our former quarters in Bordeaux, and there our time was spent most pleasantly. Our colonel was much too good a soldier to trouble those under him with unnecessary military duties, and all was gaiety and happiness.

At this time there were two or three divisions of infantry in and about the town, under the command of Marshal Beresford; but when the French troops were withdrawn from the opposite side of the river, our force was diminished and the command was vested in the Earl of Dalhousie, Marshal Beresford going with a large force to join part of the army near Toulouse.[53]

Now, I must confess – perhaps to my shame – that, despite my constant intercourse with strangers, I had then, and have still, a natural and unconquerable shyness, which made me hate to make myself known to persons, especially those above me in rank or station in the service; consequently, although I had been known to the Earl of Dalhousie from infancy, and knew him to be not only one of my father's most intimate friends, but one of the easiest men to approach, I could not make up my mind to do the correct thing and call upon him – but chance did what I would not do for myself.

One forenoon, while wandering about looking at the town, I stopped to examine some pictures in a shop window. To my horror, I saw, coming from the opposite side of the street, a general officer and his *aide-de-camp*; on the general coming up, of course, I saluted by putting my hand to my cap, which caused him in returning it, to look me in the face, on doing so his lordship exclaimed: 'William Hay!' I answered: 'The same, my lord.' Then he expressed his delight at seeing me, he had quite forgotten that my regiment was the 12th Light Dragoons, then under his immediate command. He introduced me, to his *aide-de-camp*, and made me

---

53   Lieutenant General George Ramsay, 9th Earl of Dalhousie, who commanded the Seventh Division October 1812 to October 1813 and again February to April 1814. When Beresford was recalled to the main army with the Fourth Division and Vivian's Brigade, Dalhousie was left to hold the city with his Seventh Division to which the 12th Light Dragoons, including the squadron previously left outside Bayonne, was attached to provide him with a cavalry force.

'George, Earl of Dalhousie & G.C.B.' Mezzotint by Thomas Lipton after John Watson Gordon.
(Anne S.K. Brown Military Collection)

promise to dine with him at 6 p.m.;[54] and next day a letter was received by Colonel Ponsonby expressing his lordship's desire that I should be appointed his orderly officer.

That order appeared in the garrison orders that very night. I was then inducted into my new duties, and from that hour and during the ten years I had the honour of serving the Earl of Dalhousie, nothing could exceed the kindness and consideration I experienced at the hands of that amiable nobleman. I became not only his *aide-de-camp*, but his constant companion.

For some time after receiving this new appointment I was employed in reconnoitring the country, bringing intelligence of where the enemy were posted, and such like duties.

On one occasion his lordship proposed inspecting the whole of the corps under his command, if he could find a place suitable for so large a body of men to assemble. Colonel Ralph Abercrombie was the quarter-master-general, and he and I were directed to look out and report the most convenient place to be found.[55] The place selected was a large heath, as wild as any part of Scotland, lying between two immense forests some eight or ten miles beyond the Garonne.

Preparatory to inspection the troops were ordered to assemble and form a camp on ground some miles nearer Bordeaux. Fortunately, as it turned out, artillery and three troops of dragoons formed part of the armament intended for the sham fight which was proposed to take place on the ground we had decided upon; a sufficient number of men were left behind to garrison the town of Bordeaux. The others had taken up their encamping ground, and myself, with the general and his staff, followed, putting up for the night at a neat, clean village on the main road leading to Paris.

In the morning, by a little after daylight, the different brigades were put in motion, as if expecting to meet the enemy, little dreaming that such a possibility existed near that part of the country. Cavalry patrols were formed to the front and flanks, riflemen next, and so on.

We had just mounted our horses and were proceeding along the route taken by the troops in advance, when we were met by an orderly coming from the front at a gallop. He brought a report from the senior officer to the general, stating that the advance-guard had been fired upon by a picket of the enemy, who were posted on a rising ground about two miles further on the road.

At such unexpected intelligence all looked astounded, as we did not conceive a French soldier was near. The troops were ordered to halt and form, ready to deploy into what position might become necessary. I was desired to attend the

---

54 Dalhousie's aide de camp was Captain Sir George Couper, Bart., of the 92nd Highlanders.

55 This was Lt. Colonel the Hon. Alexander – not Ralph – Abercromby, 28th Foot, a veteran of long Peninsular service including the acting command of a brigade at Albuera, who had been serving since February 1813 as Assistant Quartermaster General to the Seventh Division.

quarter-master-general, taking with me a few dragoons, for the purpose of making a patrol to the front to ascertain more accurately the state of affairs.

Sure enough, before proceeding any great distance, we came up with a body of French infantry, who had thrown out their skirmishers to occupy the thick pine-woods on each side of the road. As to the actual strength of the party by which we were opposed, it was, from the nature of the ground, difficult to ascertain; however, it was very evident we were in for a fight of some kind.[56]

On the result of our observations being made known to Lord Dalhousie, the rifle corps of his division was ordered to the front for the purpose of clearing the wood. This was done without much loss on either side.[57]

When we were able to advance we found, on the plain at the end of the road leading through the wood where it was intended we should have had the field-day, several battalions of French infantry drawn up in line, supported by a squadron of cavalry.

Evidently their surprise was as great as our own, and our appearance had been so unexpected by them, their men and officers were seen running from all parts of the wood we had just passed through, which had been their bivouac the previous night.

Having got first into the plain, with about a dozen of the 12th Dragoons, whom I had taken with me on the duty I had been sent on, I immediately charged them, when ten or twelve officers surrendered as prisoners to my small party; in fact, I found myself for some minutes surrounded by a lot of men and officers, who had thrown away their arms, suing for quarter. They were sent to the rear, and when I got back to the general and his staff, the troops had marched into position, and the French, observing that we had cavalry drawn up ready to charge, began to form squares, and, at the moment of which I speak, it was one of the most animating sights I ever beheld.

As soon as the guns were brought to bear on the French square, the 12th advanced at the charge in a most gallant style, and with the small number of men (one hundred and fifty) not only broke the first square of six hundred men who laid down their arms, but prepared to attack another body. But the general, to save so much bloodshed, had the guns brought close up, well supported by a superior force of both cavalry and infantry; so prudence was thought the better part of valour, and the French engaged agreed to lay down their arms; the remainder retired to the fortress of Blaye, to which place the whole party had been on their march when the incident I have related, intercepted it.

---

56   The action described here is that fought at Étauliers on 6 April 1814, although Hay's account exaggerates the role of the 12th Light Dragoons – of which only a squadron was present – and the numbers of prisoners taken. See Bamford, *Gallantry and Discipline*, pp.223-225.

57   This is a reference to the Brunswick-Oels Light Infantry, serving in Gardiner's Brigade of the Seventh Division: there were no actual riflemen present at this action.

I am not aware of having particularly mentioned anything about my own conduct in the affair that deserved commendation; but it so met the appreciation of my general, that he not only wrote a kind and handsome letter to his friend – my father – stating a most flattering opinion of me, but requested permission from the Duke of Wellington to be allowed to appoint me as his extra *aide-de-camp*, an honour, I assure you, which not a little gratified my pride.

After a few days' sojourn in the neighbourhood of the citadel of Blaye, we returned to Bordeaux, and a few days after fought the battle of Toulouse. That was followed up by the arrival of an officer, Colonel Cook – from the Allied Armies of Russia, Austria, and Prussia – bearer of despatches to the Duke of Wellington, notifying the abdication of Bonaparte. So ended our fighting for a time.

For a while we had ample time to rest and amuse ourselves. Quartered in a delightful town, full of our own officers, both naval and military, theatres every night, and pleasure parties every day.

Amongst other French officers, I made the acquaintance of, was the Marquis de Laroche-jaquelein, who came forward prominently at the restoration – having raised an independent corps of royalists – and I spent many happy hours in his company, both at his own chateaux in the country and his lodgings in Bordeaux, hearing him relate his extraordinary adventures and escapes.[58] Among his officers was a good-natured country gentleman, the Count de — (I forget his name), who had managed, through all his misfortune, to live in his chateau about ten miles out of Bordeaux, in a sort of splendid state. The house was in a dilapidated condition, the faded remnants of what had been, in former days, grandeur. He was a keen sportsman, and was commonly known by the name of the 'Chasseur'; and had continued, in all his distress, to keep a pack of hounds of the long, slow breed, in which he took the greatest pride. He, a brother *aide-de-camp* of mine – Lord Hay – and myself soon became sworn friends, as we were both sportsmen as well as the Frenchman.

(By this time I may observe, I had become a full *aide-de-camp*, and Hay had taken my place as extra.)[59]

---

58 This was Louis, marquis de La Rochejaquelein, whose elder brother had been a noted general of the Vendéen Royalists in the 1790s. Louis would command the *Compagnie des Grenadiers à Cheval du Roi* after the restoration, and was killed during the Hundred Days when the Vendée again rose in arms for the Bourbons. See John R Elting, *Swords Around A Throne: Napoleon's Grande Armée* (London: Weidenfeld and Nicolson, 1989), pp.632, 663, 660.

59 This was in consequence of the departure of Couper to take up a staff post in North America. The new extra aide de camp was Ensign James, Lord Hay, 1st Foot Guards, not to be confused with Captain Lord James Hay of the same regiment, encountered earlier in this narrative as an aide de camp to Sir Stapleton Cotton. Lord Hay had been commissioned the previous October and had only arrived in the Peninsula shortly before the end of hostilities. He was killed at Quatre Bras whilst serving as an aide de camp to Sir Peregrine Maitland, and appears, in heavily-fictionalised form, as one of the main characters in the 1970 film *Waterloo*.

To his house we frequently repaired either to shoot or hunt. The chasseur's dress, when equipped for the chase, consisted of a green suit, richly embroidered, a large gilt chain round his shoulders to which was appended a huge bugle-horn, of French make, large boots, and an enormous cocked hat. He was wretchedly mounted, and his great ambition was to possess himself of an English horse and equipments.

I happened at the time to have a very hot mare and hard puller, indeed so difficult to ride that no one but myself, who was acquainted with the brute's ways, would think of getting on her back. This mare I rode one day when out with our friend's hounds.

She was, to look at, a splendid animal, and, as a Frenchman always imagines he can do anything better than any one else, he admired her and wanted to purchase or exchange anything he had for her. I told him she would break his neck, on which he was most indignant, declaring he could ride much better than any Englishman, and that I was only afraid of exposing how much better he could manage a hot horse than I could. On this subject I kept him so much excited, that he did not reflect on the distance he had come from his own chateau on the road to town in his most extraordinary costume.

When getting to the point, I determined to indulge in a bit of fun at the expense of the count. I whispered my plan to my friend, who highly approved.

It may have been about 3 p.m., the time when the different officers in garrison turned out to ride. We met many of our acquaintances, who not only enjoyed a chat with us about the sport, but looked with wonder and amazement on the dress of the count who was with us. When about a dozen of us had collected, ready for any lark, I proposed to the count to try the mare, to which he readily consented. Off I got, and altered the leathers to the Frenchman's length, slipped the last chain of the bridle off the hooks into my own pocket, got him fairly mounted, and jumped on his hack.

He went off like a shot, the whole party at his heels; through the holloaing and whipping behind, the mare became quite unmanageable, he kept his seat, like John Gilpin;[60] but as to guiding the mare, he never made the attempt, therefore she took the lead at full speed with a straight run into the town, and for about two miles bang through the streets we went, the great bugle swinging about his head and his tormentors in the rear, to the astonishment of all good people.

Our friend kept his seat until he reached the gate of the chateau which constituted the headquarters of the commander-in-chief. To the surprise of the sentry, through the gate he went, and right up to the stable door, which most fortunately, for the head or legs of the chasseur, was shut.

---

60   The eponymous hero of the 1782 comic ballad *The Diverting History of John Gilpin* by William Cowper, who was also carried away by a runway horse.

When we came up, we found him addressing the grooms on the '*Sacre bete,*' he had been mounted on, but I must, in justice to him, say no man ever took anything in better humour than he did that gallop. He thought our flying after him was with a view of rendering assistance; he was covered with dust and perspiration, and such a sight as few ever have had the satisfaction of witnessing.

When standing in the saddle-room, to recover himself, and chatting about his feats of horsemanship, I said, to make amends for his ride, if he would undertake to allow himself to be saddled, and a bridle put round his neck, and, in that form, carry them to Larochejaquelein's (his commanding officer) lodgings, I would let him take his choice of any horse he might fix on, and keep it for so doing.

He was quite agreeable to the proposal; and when a groom was employed to saddle and bridle him and others kept him in conversation, I slipped out, cautioned the soldiers on guard what was to take place, ordered them to let him pass a certain distance as if unobserved, and then send a file of men to bring him back prisoner for stealing the general's saddlery.

Out he went fully equipped, and had got about a hundred yards when captured, and was expostulating with the soldiers, when, who should come up but Lord Dalhousie himself. He was speechless for some time with laughing; but it turned out a profitable thing for the chasseur, as the good, kind earl placed at my disposal, to present to our friend, two English mares and two saddles and bridles, which made the chasseur a very proud and happy man, and quite made up for all the tricks we had played upon him.

Bordeaux was by this time filled with English troops, and a large camp was formed in the neighbourhood, composed of regiments about to embark for America, and others to return home. My own regiment, the 12th Dragoons, had taken its departure to march through the country to Calais.

There was one other man, besides the chasseur, with whom we had formed an acquaintance, whom I must also tell a tale about. He was a Father Burk, a tall, raw-boned, old Irish priest, who had settled years before at Bordeaux, and, I do believe, as great a villain as ever lived unhanged; he not only dealt in his own wares, of selling absolution – but had taken up a sort of trade as a retailer of wine, which wine he had probably extracted from the poor in hearing confession, etc.

This man was the greatest intruder. He came at all hours and times to Government House and, to our annoyance, listened to and repeated everything he heard the *aides-de-camp* talking about in the waiting-room. So to show him up in some way was our ambition, and an opportunity occurred.

The quarter-master-general, a great friend of mine, was about to leave the 7th division and embark for America with the Army destined for that country.[61] Burk had contrived to work his way into his good graces, was a constant visitor at his

61   This was Abercromby; however, there is no reference to his having served in North America.

house, and made himself useful in obtaining wines of different kinds to suit the taste of his indulgent and kind host.

The order to take up his appointment was very sudden, and little time given for his preparations; he deputed me to do several things for him that time would not allow his doing for himself. Burk happened to be present when he heard the commissions given me on various subjects, amongst others was to see that some wine he had bought was shipped for England.

A town at the mouth of the river, called Pauillac, was the place where the troops assembled and embarked, about forty miles from Bordeaux.

Abercrombie had taken his leave, and departed for the above named place, and I knew he was to embark and sail immediately, the wind being fair, therefore I set to work and wrote myself a letter, as if from Abercrombie, dated Pauillac, stating, in his hurry, he had quite forgotten to order, from his good friend Father Burk, some wine that he had been in the habit of obtaining from him; and for that purpose he enclosed me a letter which he wished me to give him on the subject, giving full instructions to whom it was to be consigned in London, etc., etc., and enclosing in it an order for the amount. The epistle to Burk certainly gave most full directions, and had in it three Bills of Exchange, purporting to be worth £100, at least a third more than we knew the wine was worth, requesting the good father to keep the change as his own commission, and many other civil things were said. The bills were drawn out, and signed in a business like-manner, and directed to the 'The Pump at Aldgate,'

Early in the morning an orderly was sent to Burk's house with the despatch. (I must here observe one thing: with all old Burk's native cunning he was a most illiterate animal, and I have my doubts if he could read writing – at all events, I am sure not without difficulty.)

The hour of his usual visiting arrived, and we sat in expectation of his coming very angry, of course supposing he would see through the joke at once. But no; Father Burk made his appearance later in the evening, and I told him I had heard from Abercrombie who had sent a message for him. He exclaimed: 'Have I not heard myself, and is he not the best and most liberal gentleman that ever lived?' Here he produced the letter with the greatest satisfaction, said he had been to order the wine to be got ready and put into double cases, and had been so busy all the morning executing that and other commissions for his good friend the colonel, as he called him.

We were perfectly astonished to see how well our bait had taken, and at the man's stupidity; however, we enjoyed it all too much to, in any way, mar the proceedings. He left the room delighted with the task of the morning.

Next day he came with a very different face, and in the most awful rage, demanded an audience of the earl. We tried to prevent that, but it was of no use, he would hear no explanation, and the noise he made brought the general into the room to see what was the matter. He then laid before his lordship the whole business, showing him the pretended letter and the Bills of Exchange, said he would be ruined, as he had ordered the wine, and when he took the bills to sell them on 'change,' he was laughed at by all the merchants. (The old man was hated by all the townspeople, so it was nuts to them when the report got wind.)

Lord Dalhousie had to run out of the room and shut himself in his own, as he laughed to such a degree hearing Burk's account of the whole transaction. It had one good effect, he was so offended he never came to the house again.

In the earlier part of these notes you may recollect a person I mentioned, as having learned how to forage for his dinner, when marching a country like Portugal, by killing stray sheep and living in priests' houses![62] That same individual happened at this time to arrive at Bordeaux on his way to join the Army going to America. He, as a matter of course, came to see me, the hour he called was near dinner-time, we were very punctual and I was rather late in going to my room, where he followed me; he kept walking about the room talking while I was dressing and so much engaged as not to observe his motions. He said: 'Hay, how do I look?' On casting my eyes to where he was standing, with the handle of the door in his hand, to my surprise he was fully dressed in my uniform: sash, hat, etc., etc.! I said: 'Oh, very well!' 'Then good morning,' said he, leaving the room and locking the door on the outside, merely uttering as I rushed to prevent him: 'Recollect the pass of Villa Valle.'

The French houses had no bells in those days, and mine happened to be a very large room in a part of the house by itself, so – as I could make no one hear until a servant was sent to know what prevented my coming down to dinner – there I remained. The laugh was now turned much against me, but I could say nothing; having enjoyed so many at the expense of others, it was quite fair my own turn should come.

Our truly delightful sojourn at Bordeaux was drawing to a close, the troops were assembled about fifty miles down the river to be near the ships to convey them to England. And, notwithstanding it was the month of July, with a South of France sun, the general for some time rode to the place of embarkation every day, on which occasions I always accompanied him, making a hundred miles a day; and most days a party of twenty or more to entertain to dinner on getting home. We had relays of horses on the road, which was deep sand, and we galloped the whole distance.

I was still young, being under twenty, therefore, to me, it ought to be no great exertion; but I have often wondered since how Lord Dalhousie could have sustained it, having so many other points on military matters to attend to, besides a large correspondence home, so both his body and mind were kept in constant exertion.

Towards the end of July the guards, who were the last troops to leave the shores of France, having all embarked, we took our departure from Bordeaux, which, notwithstanding the prospect of returning to my native land after some years'

---

62   This, of course, was De Lacy Evans.

absence, I did with great regret. I am very certain that never before or since have I spent so truly a happy time as I did in that delightful city.

The Earl of Dalhousie and his staff, with a battalion of the guards, adjutant, quarter-master-general, and other officers, went on board the *Montague* commanded by a most agreeable and gentlemanly captain, called Haywood.[63]

After a short and pleasant voyage we arrived at Spithead, dined with the commandant of Portsmouth, and proceeded next morning to London, breakfasting on our way with Lord Keith, and remained in the metropolis some days to put our clothes into some sort of order. I accompanied his lordship to Scotland and took leave of him at Dunbar, where we arrived about seven in the morning. I there found some of my sisters awaiting my arrival, and met with the usual kind reception from my beloved father and mother. On my last leaving them their dread was the state of my health; but God had not only spared me, but enabled me to bear with all the privations and hardships, recover my health, and return without a complaint.

---

63 There are some slight spelling errors here: the ship was HMS *Montagu*, a 74-gun third rate launched in 1779 and now coming to the end of a career that had included action at the Saintes and Camperdown. Her commanding officer was Captain Peter Heywood, whose 'agreeable and gentlemanly' exterior belied an extraordinary career. As a midshipman he had been a participant in the infamous *Bounty* mutiny and had lived for some years as a fugitive on Tahiti before being brought back to Britain to face a court martial that sentenced him to death. Pardoned thanks to his family connections whereas the majority of his lower-deck co-accused met with the noose, he subsequently resumed his naval career and served with distinction in the wars against France.

3

The Hundred Days and After

The short time allowed me to remain at home was spent as happily as days generally are in visiting and being visited by friends and neighbours. During the time I was at home I made one grand mistake, and I have observed through life from after experience, if a man once refuses the tide of prosperity, when it seems to float him along, he seldom, if ever, recovers his ground again, and it was the case with me.

My father and his family at this time had the honour of the acquaintance, as a neighbour, of one of the most enlightened, generous, and kind-hearted of noblemen, and his family, the late Earl of Lauderdale, who resided at Dunbar House, and I was a frequent guest. His lordship's influence with the then commander-in-chief, the Duke of York, was well known, he most kindly and condescendingly, without having previously informed either my father or myself of his intention, used it on my behalf in obtaining His Royal Highness's permission to present me with a company in the 44th regiment. On his lordship informing my father, the over-indulgent parent asked permission to consult me, which he did on returning home, after having dined at Dunbar House.

My predilection for my old companions of the 12th got the better of my senses, and I preferred to remain as lieutenant and re-join them. So ended the year 1814, and my prospects of promotion for some years to come.

About February, 1815, my staff appointment, as *aide-de-camp* to Lord Dalhousie, ceased.

My kind father made me a present of two splendid horses as chargers, and full equipments for them and myself, and I took my departure for Dorchester, at which place my regiment was quartered at the time. It was the most horrid, dull, stupid inland town I had ever known. I may say that, until then, I never knew what it was to lead, what is commonly termed, a barrack-yard life.

We had hunting, it is true, of an indifferent kind; and an old fellow, a yeoman farmer, who at the time was an Army contractor to supply the cavalry regiments in the place with forage, gave us some amusement in his meadows, where we used to hunt rats, to pass the dull hours.

Towards spring corn had reached a high price, bread was dear, and the restless disposition of the people became roused by the sudden change that had taken place, from a long and protracted war; symptoms of disturbance, in and about London, were the consequences. Troops were ordered to the neighbourhood and others to hold themselves in readiness to march for the metropolis; in the latter case was the 12th Dragoons, I for one was delighted at the prospect of breaking ground from Dorchester, be our destination where it would.

Under such orders our mess establishment was broken up, and we dined at the inn; there was but one in the place and to that the mail-coach was driven on its arrival. The officers were waiting the sounding of trumpets for dinner, at the said inn door, when the mail stopped. The guard, a good-humoured fellow and a great favourite with all our officers, who had travelled to town by his coach, exclaimed: 'Well, gentlemen, I have brought you news to-day.' All exclaimed: 'What! the route?' 'Yes,' was the reply, 'the route in earnest, old Bonny [sic] has broken out again and got to Paris.' We were astonished, and indeed could not believe our ears; but on the delivery of the newspapers and letters the news we heard was not only confirmed, but an immediate order for us to march by Canterbury, *en route* to Dover, there to embark for Ostend, and, I must confess, the news gave me the greatest satisfaction, as I had no liking for the life of a soldier in idleness.

We got together our campaigning equipage once more, our heavy baggage was ordered into stores. I took with me a handsome setter, one of a brace, a parting gift from my father, I mention him as he will be mentioned as a travelling companion later on in the expedition. On our arrival at Canterbury the regiment was inspected by General Pack, and next day we marched to our different places of embarkation.[1]

The troop I was attached to went to Dover, sailing that afternoon for Ostend, where we arrived in due course.[2] From thence we went by easy stages, in the first place to the neighbourhood of Brussels, ultimately taking up our quarters in some villages about thirty miles from the capital. Our time was passed, as is usually the case with officers in country quarters in a foreign land, going about to see what was worthy of observation, within our reach.

The Marquis of Anglesea [sic] commanded the cavalry, and his natural anxiety was to have them, as a body, as efficient as his ardent and able spirit could make them; therefore, about twice each week, the whole, to the number of about ten thousand men, assembled for field-day exercise; it formed a splendid sight from the village where our headquarters were stationed.[3]

1   The inspection took place on 1 April; see regimental orders of 31 March 1815 in 9th/12th Royal Lancers Regimental Museum, Derby, 912L:2088/5 "12th Lancers Order Book 1815-1872", pp.1-2.
2   The troop to which Hay was assigned was that commanded by Captain George Francis Erskine, and in turn formed one half of the Left Squadron. Since Erskine had command of the squadron in action by virtue of being its senior captain, Hay would have been left with the direction of the troop.
3   The seven brigades of British and KGL cavalry, along with a single brigade of Hanoverians, were grouped along with their supporting artillery as a single Cavalry Corps – in effect an oversized division – under the command of Lieutenant General the Earl of Uxbridge, who was not created Marquis of Anglesey until after, and in recognition of his services during, the Waterloo campaign. The 12th Light

The distance to the ground cannot have been less than twenty-five miles, therefore, during the very hot weather experienced in June, that was severe work; consequently, I did not care to move far from home on rest days, and refused a very pressing invitation to attend the ball given by his Grace the Duke of Richmond the evening previous to the battle of Quatre Bras.[4]

In the morning of the June 16, 1815, about 3 a.m., my servant came into my room and was arranging my clothes, when, half-asleep, I exclaimed: 'Is it so near the time for marching already?' His reply was, 'We are going to march in earnest; the field-day is countermanded, and the colonel, who has this moment arrived from Brussels, wishes to see you at his house immediately.'

I jumped out of bed and over to Colonel Ponsonby's quarters. His first exclamation was, 'You were lucky not to go to the ball, I am quite knocked up, the French are coming on in great numbers, and yesterday attacked and drove the Prussians back! Tell the sergeant to give orders for three days' rations and forage to be served immediately; and as soon as that is done, the order to be given for the regiment to march. I should like to be left quiet, as long as possible, to get some rest.'[5]

I performed my instructions; and that day we halted fifty-two miles from where we started in the morning. (I shall, in some degree, deviate from my rule laid down at the commencement of this account of my own proceedings, by giving, perhaps, a more detailed description of the general movements of the Army during June 16, 17, and 18 than may, from my previous observations, seem altogether consistent.)

However, from the experience I had obtained in the service as an infantry, dragoon, and staff officer engaged in different branches of my profession, and in most of the battles and affairs that took place from the retreat of the Army after the battle on the heights of Busaco, in 1810, till the present period, may, I hope, plead some excuse for attempting to entertain you with what my own ideas were on the points on which I had ocular demonstration, and how and where I was prominently engaged during those three momentous days in British and French history.

Dragoons formed part of the 4th Cavalry Brigade along with the 11th and 16th Light Dragoons, the brigadier being Major General Sir John Ormsby Vandeleur, a distant cousin of the 12th's lieutenant of that name, who had also commanded the brigade composed of the 12th and 16th Light Dragoons in the closing stages of the Peninsular War.

4   Hay is stretching the truth somewhat here: his name does not appear upon the list of those invited, and as a junior regimental officer of no great social standing this is hardly to be wondered at. The famous ball of 15 June was, of course, given by the Duchess of Richmond and not her husband.

5   Although invited, Lt. Colonel Ponsonby apparently chose not to attend the ball, having been alerted to the skirmishing along the frontier earlier in the day. See Major General Sir John Ponsonby, *The Ponsonby Family*. (London: Medici Society, 1929), p.119. Hay would seem to be again embroidering his narrative.

We marched from our quarters at Volsel at about 6 a.m., with directions to assemble in brigade at the town of d'Enghien on the main road between Brussels and Paris, the point of assembly for several corps that had been cantoned in and about that part of the country. There we arrived about nine o'clock, and our horses were ordered to be fed with corn.[6]

In a grove of trees, near where we had halted during the operation, while waiting for orders, I wandered to where some of the battalions of guards were forming, and there found a party of old friends and acquaintances going to breakfast. I was, as a matter of course, invited to join them, but, having already breakfasted, I threw myself on the grass to enjoy their company and a chat on the prospects of the work preparing for the Army.

I have frequently brought to my mind that party on account of the sudden and melancholy separation of those of whom it consisted. The number was nine.

I happened somehow or other to have torn my trousers, and one of our companions said in joke: 'I know who expects to be killed to-day' On being asked whom he meant, he pointed to my rent garment, laughing, but strangely enough I was the only one on the evening of those three eventful days who was untouched: six were killed, or died of their wounds, one of the others had his arm amputated, and the eighth was most desperately wounded. I saw him on what his medical man thought his death-bed the day of the battle after Waterloo, and was charged by him with, what he conceived to be, a last message to his brother.

At d'Enghien we remained till nearly twelve o'clock, awaiting orders; the road was literally choked with troops, artillery, and ammunition, going to the front, and, as cavalry was much required in the struggle that had commenced in the neighbourhood of Quatre Bras, our brigade, to clear itself of the moving impedimenta on the highway, was directed to separate and to be led through unfrequented paths by the commanding officer of each regiment, to meet at a given rendezvous, fixed on by the quarter-master-general.

The 12th, led by the active and intelligent Colonel Ponsonby, soon got clear of the difficulties that barred their progress, and we moved at a sharp pace the last ten miles before we again gained the main road, by the rear of the regiments, at a hand gallop. About that time we had got within hearing distance of the guns in front, and began to meet wounded soldiers being carried to the rear.

I am certain I do myself nothing but justice when I declare I never knew what it was to feel nervous in my life at the idea of a fight; but all must have felt an indescribable awe at witnessing, in cold blood, the sufferings of others-on these points one's feelings do not become hardened. I never entered action in my life

6   Hay's 'Volsel' cannot be located, but the 12th Light Dragoons were garrisoned around Grammont (in Flemish, Geraardsbergen), some 25 miles west of Brussels. It is unclear why Hay has chosen to add the preposition to the name of Enghien; possibly the name was more familiar to him with that addition in the context of the unfortunate duc d'Enghien, shot on the orders of Napoleon in 1804.

without asking, in a few words of humble petition, the Almighty Dispenser of all good to bestow on me the power to do my duty; and, from the instant those words were uttered, I felt myself moved to capability of any performance that might be required of either my mind or body.

If those of my companions of days gone by heard me acknowledge this, they would probably say they did not give me credit for such serious thoughts, as, I believe, I made as little outward show of religion as any man living; but I never forgot the principles instilled into me at home, and in all my undertakings placed the fullest confidence in the goodness and power of God, and in those trying times, and since, I have had extended to me His many kindnesses and mercies in many ways I am not able to express.

I have, though, somewhat wandered from my subject. We emerged to the right hand taking a lane, or cross-road, which led towards the plain on which the two Armies had been at such deadly work all the morning. On getting into the ground we formed into squadrons, and, having advanced in echelon, at a gallop for some distance along the plain, we formed line, fronting the enemy, who were at the time returning from the field of action then covered by their artillery, which gave us a few shots of salutation. However, it was not deemed advisable to take part against them.[7]

On our coming to a halt Colonel Ponsonby beckoned me to follow him, and we went to where the highland regiment had been charged by the cuirassiers while in the act of forming into squares.[8] After the many actions and fields covered with dead and dying I had witnessed, it was, I thought, no novel sight to me; but the number of men and horses lying there far exceeded anything I could have formed any conception of. The ground bore evident marks of what a struggle had taken place, and how truly gallantly and bravely my countrymen must have acted their part in the unequal strife.

I was rendered speechless with wonder, when the voice of Colonel Ponsonby called me to my senses by telling me to look at a cuirass he had taken from one of the dead bodies-it was perforated with three balls. He said: 'I wanted to find out if these cuirasses were ball proof or not, this plainly shows they are not.' On looking closely I pointed out several others with one or two balls through them. Having satisfied ourselves on the subject we returned to the regiment. Evening was now closing in, but that brought no rest for us. Cavalry regiments, who,

---

7   The fighting at Quatre Bras had begun to die down around 21.00, so if Hay's memory is to be relied on then the brigade must have arrived on the field a little after that. If he did come under fire, it most have been from random 'overs' but even this would seem unlikely at this time of day. For the close of the action and the state of the field at this time, see Mike Robinson, *The Battle of Quatre Bras 1815* (Stroud: The History Press, 2009) p.357-361.

8   The charge of the 8e and 11e Cuirassiers, supported by French light cavalry, was broadly up the axis of the Charleroi-Brussels road, with the square of the 42nd Royal Highlanders being just to the east of the Chaussée. See Robinson, *Quatre Bras*, pp.310-322.

like ourselves, had come from a distance, kept arriving on the ground, and as every succeeding brigade made its appearance ours took ground to the left. This continued throughout the night.

On such occasions it is odd enough, I have no doubt, to those who have not undergone such fatigue, to hear of constant day and night work without being quite knocked up, but it really is the case, that one does not even feel tired. For my own part, I had been so long in the habit of doing duty on the outposts, snatching a few moments' sleep on the least opportunity, that as soon as the halt sounded I was off my horse and asleep like a dog in a minute; consequently, I was always fresh night and day. When covering guns and stationary in action I often did the same thing.

The heavy tread of the march of infantry, the rattling of the swords of the dragoons, and the noise of the wheels of guns and ammunition-waggons, intermixed with the bugle and trumpets during the whole night, portend active preparations for the forthcoming day; all, I may affirm, had such implicit faith in their great leader that no concern was felt as to the movements made.

Soon after the dawn of day I had an opportunity of observing the country near us; it was an irregular, wild-looking tract, mostly uncultivated, here and there a patch of land with corn on it and a house, but mostly covered with short grass and ferns, surrounded on three sides by woods, two of which appeared of impenetrable thickness – these were at the further end of the plain of which I speak.

We had moved during the night to the extreme left of our Army towards the roads leading to Quatre Bras, through Waterloo to Brussels.

I could descry but few of our troops, with the exception of the cavalry; the artillery were all in motion in the rear of our lines; and the infantry evidently changing from position to position in a retiring movement; it struck me as odd, but I well knew it was no business of mine and must have been for some grand purpose; not an enemy was to be seen.

About one o'clock in the day the last of the infantry had disappeared. The cavalry, about ten thousand in number, had the ground to themselves and commenced concentrating from different parts of the former position occupied by the Army on the previous day and night, to which they had been detached in brigades, and were now drawn up evidently on a well selected piece of ground to cover the roads by which the artillery and infantry were retiring.

The cavalry were formed into four lines, composed of first, the pickets, who may have been at the distance of one and half miles in front and flank; second, the hussar brigade and some light dragoons; third, the heavy dragoons; fourth, light dragoons, of whose last line the 12th formed part.

The lay of the ground on which we were drawn up was a slight incline descending towards the great plain in our front; on the enclosures and broken woodland, through which the roads mentioned ran, the lines rested. I commanded the left squadron, and from the nature of the ground had an excellent and uninterrupted view of all my front.[9] The morning had been sultry and black and heavy clouds indicated a thunder-storm.

From where we stood to the extreme boundary of the forest that surrounded the plain may have been about two miles. Through that forest three great avenues, or main roads, ran, coming from different points towards the open, as it appeared. At a great distance in the wood, on each side of those roads, clouds of dust began to spread over the trees. That dust approached thicker and thicker, and dead silence pervaded our ranks, I thought even the horses were more still than usual, no champing of bits, no clattering of swords. Every eye was directed anxiously to what was passing in the front.

In a moment, as if by magic, debouched from the dark green foliage, which had hitherto kept them from our sight, by the three roads, the gorgeous uniforms of the French cavalry, composed of the cuirassiers, lancers, and brass-helmeted dragoons. On they came at a gallop, those from the right-hand road forming on the plain to their left, the centre to their front, and the left to their right, until three lines fronting our own were drawn up. There were now in front of us, waiting, twenty-two thousand (22,000) cavalry – double our number – and these supported by fifty guns of artillery, all ready for action.

Although one may imagine the feeling of excitement at the moment, when looking at so truly splendid a sight – one of real grandeur – I will answer for it, at least for the truly gallant men under my command, the ardent desire was to be allowed to charge them. The reckless, unsteady soldier, when under the discipline of adjutants' drill in the barrack-yard, was, at such a time, as steady as a rock, anxious to be guided by his officer, the glance of whose eye was responded to, and ready to move or stand as directed. I must say I felt proud when I looked down the ranks of my own half squadron, as I knew every man from long experience, and could tell what at the moment was passing in their minds, when returning my look, as the word 'Steady men' was given.

The enemy, having satisfied himself as to the perfection of his formation and advance parties being ordered to take the lead, the onward march began; but how utterly powerless with all their efforts, are the endeavours of men, when even compared with the very drops of water sent by God from heaven, was truly demonstrated on this occasion!

The clouds which had been gathering for some time in blackness, as striving to contrast their colour and thickness with the clouds of white dust driven upwards, suddenly burst, and one of the most awful storms of thunder and lightning I ever beheld, opened a battery.

---

9   Hay was too junior for a squadron command. What he was in fact commanding was the left-most of the two troops that made up the Left Squadron of the regiment, something that he actually confirms himself a little later in his narrative.

The enemy's lines began to close with ours, and when within a short distance, as if a sluice-gate had been opened, down came such torrents of rain as quite obliterated from our view even our own advance, this continued with such violence in our teeth, that our position seemed untenable; our horses with spurs stuck in their flanks would not keep their heads to the storm.

The word of command was now given to retire by divisions from the left, therefore I was first to move off the ground we occupied, first at a walk, then a trot. I well knew the difficulty of leading a long line of followers either in advance or retreat, and therefore wished to move at a slow pace, but I soon found my tactics were of no use in this instance as the ward was constantly piped 'faster, faster, in front.'

As soon as we had cleared the ground, on which we had been drawn up, our way lay by a narrow cross-country road, full of holes and of broad, deep ruts full of water from the recent rains. Along this road was most horrid riding, on account of the nature of the soil, which was a stiff slippery clay; consequently, the crowding from the rear pushed many men and their horses into the deep ditches by the road side.

From former days' experience I well knew the difficulty to be encountered in flying an enemy, and to get your own men in order again when you would stop – a front movement soon meets its own level. Therefore I was glad when joined by Ponsonby, who had jostled past somehow from the rear of the regiment. By this time the rain was not nearly so violent and the storm subsiding gradually.

On coming to the end of the road, perhaps some four miles from where we started, we came to a more open country. Looking towards a small inclining plain was a large open space on our left, on this space the colonel ordered me to form up the squadron.

While the dragoons were getting ready, I glanced round at the country in our immediate front, which I saw was occupied by troops in dark dresses, and on observing their movements attentively, I saw guns move into position, begin to unlimber, and make ready to open fire on our column. I, of course, took them for French, not having the slightest idea of the part of the country we were in at the moment.

I made the remark to the colonel: 'We shall catch it in another minute.' He asked me what I meant, I pointed to the guns; he took my glasses, and, on looking through them for a moment, said: 'They take *us* for *French!* Go immediately and undeceive them'; on turning to obey his orders, I said: 'If *they* are not French, what on earth *are* they?' On telling me they were *Dutch*, he undeceived me also.

On galloping towards them with one dragoon, I was met by a young officer and some dozen men, who came up as if he intended to eat me at a mouthful! He pulled out his pistol, cocked it, and held it to my head, ordering me to halt. I said I would do so if he would send one of his men and stop the guns from firing on the English troops coming into the opposite fields.

For some time the young fellow, being so excited, could not understand me; however, after various foolish and vexatious questions, he became convinced, and did as I required him, at the same time lowering his pistol and, asking my pardon for his mistake, pulled from his holster a large Dutch flask filled with brandy, begged that I would pledge him in a pull from that pistol, observing that after such a mistake it would do good. Although I never touch spirits, I was on this occasion well pleased with the change, as the chances were ten to one against me at one time, he seemed so nervous and excited.[10]

Our brigade halted for some time on the ground which formed the extreme right of the French frontier, that night and the following morning. On retiring for the night we took position where it was intended, by his grace the commander-in-chief, the extreme left of his Army should be stationed. The country around was covered with growing crops of wheat and rye in full ear, and, from the rain that had fallen and the height of the corn, it was like riding through a pond. To avoid the inconvenience, as much as circumstances would permit, we halted on the road, the brigade formed by regiments in columns of squadrons at quarter distance, the men were dismounted but ordered to keep their horses in hand to be ready at a moment's notice.

From the well arranged plan of our great commander, the Army all seemed to be in their places and making ready to repel any attack when it pleased the enemy. The infantry employed themselves in drying and cleaning their muskets after the wetting of the morning. As to lying down to rest, it was out of the question, as the road was knee deep in mud and water; consequently, the night was spent uncomfortably. We heard, the whole night long the moving of the French troops into position. Fires we had none, from lack of fuel, so the camps looked more dull than usual.

For my own part, towards morning I was so worn out with fatigue, I took my chance, and, laying my cloak on the highest ridge of mud I could find, I took my place on it, and never slept sounder in the best bed. When I was awakened by my companions about 6 a.m. I found myself in rather a strange plight, having sunk some six or eight inches deep in the water and clay. However, our attentive sutler had arrived from the rear and brought with him a good breakfast which put us all in good spirits.

To make what I may afterwards state more explicit, I may as well give the best idea I can of the nature of the ground on which so great a contest was about to take place. The length from one end to the other, *i.e.*, from right to left, I do not think exceeded three miles if so much, the breadth not two miles. From about the right centre of the British position was a gentle slope in the ground, at some points a

---

10 This was possibly the Netherlands battery commanded by Capt. Emanuel Stevenaar, which ultimately ended up well to the left when the army redeployed at Waterloo and so could have conceivably been encountered by the 4th Cavalry Brigade as it withdrew towards its assigned position on that same flank. If so, it is not to be wondered that the gunners were jumpy, for the battery had been badly cut up at Quatre Bras where it had lost its commanding officer and several of its guns.

little more abrupt than others, which slope ended on a flat bottom of about three hundred yards broad at the widest place. Rather to the right hand side of this flat ran a deep lane, and, on the British side, close to that lane were some low hedges and small enclosures occupied by an infantry brigade.

On the French side of the flat, the ground just opposite was rather more bold; the land lying in a considerable degree more on a slope; on the French's left of this was a flat valley, again a gentle rise in the lay of the land towards the extreme left of the enemy's position. At the top of the slopes, on each side, the country was open and pretty equal and covered with standing corn, this was, on the commencement of the morning of June 18, very high.

During the time the officers were partaking of the good things provided by the sutler – Mr. Fancois – a certain number of dragoons belonging to each troop were ordered to unbridle and feed their horses. The rain, which had continued in a more or less degree throughout the night, had now ceased, and the morning was cool and very dull. We sat watching the proceedings in the enemy's camp on the rising ground opposite us with, I may say, intense anxiety – when the first gun or guns were fired by them, from a height nearly in front of the left centre of the British position – as nearly as I could judge.

That signal put us all in active motion, 'Bridle up and stand to your horses!' was the order.

Bugles, trumpets, and beating of drums, 'To Arms!' was the order of the moment throughout the whole line.

We mounted instantly, and formed into line of regiments – left in front – which gave the 12th the lead into action, when the time arrived.[11]

The first orders which reached our brigade, were to move from their station and extend towards their left – which I considered was given with a view to keep up communication with the advance of the Prussians, which Army it was hoped might be approaching – however we had not proceeded far in that direction, when another staff-officer came with orders for us to retrace our steps, which we did at a sharp pace in open column of squadrons, the left still leading. When we arrived in this order, on the left flank of our infantry, which formed the left centre, and were at the time occupying the hedges and broken ground on the right of the deep lane, before mentioned, we were halted for a moment.[12]

---

11   As the second most senior regiment in the brigade, the 12th Light Dragoons took the second place of honour, on the far left flank. For more on the role of seniority in troop formations, see Howie Muir, "Order of Battle: Customary Battle-Array in Wellington's Peninsular Army", in Rory Muir et al, *Inside Wellington's Peninsular Army 1808-1814* (Barnsley: Pen and Sword, 2006), pp.84-171.

12   This infantry would have been the Landwehr battalions of the 4th and 5th Hanoverian Brigades, commanded respectively by Colonels Charles Best and Ernst von Vincke. This movement by the 4th Cavalry Brigade was carried out on the initiative of its commander, Major General Vandeleur, in order to provide support to the troops being driven back by the attack of the French I Corps. The subsequent

Through one of those small enclosures was a narrow open space leading into the flat between the sloping ground on each side.

During the few minutes allowed us while halted, I observed, on our left, three or four squares of French infantry were drawn up at the bottom of the ridge and ending with their rear up the sloping ground in their front, which was covered thickly with skirmishers employed in firing across the lane at our infantry, who were returning the compliment from behind the small enclosures. On their side, behind the French squares, was artillery vomiting actual showers of grape shot and shells.

Through the small opening, or sort of gateway, I was directed, as the officer commanding the leading half squadron, to take my men. The colonel's orders were to form as soon as I had allowed for sufficient space for the whole squadron to get clear of the defile. When on the ground, I am sure I do not exaggerate when I state, as the left-hand man of the squadron, I did not sit on my horse further from the nearest French square than eighty yards; so near was I that I never thought for a moment we could have been brought there for any other purpose than to charge the square.[13]

So much was I impressed with this idea that, when the colonel placed himself in the centre of the square to lead into action, and the word of command 'Forward' given, I gave the word 'Right shoulders forward,' and in a second more would have dashed at the square next me, when I heard called out to me '*Not* that, *not* that, Hay!' I then, for the first time, discovered just in our front were moving on to the flat ground several squadrons of the French cavalry composed of lancers and light dragoons; we had no time for reflection. On we went at a gallop, sweeping past, and close to the muskets of the French, and over the skirmishers, who were running in all directions back to seek shelter.

You may conceive how close I was when I state that a man ran out and put his musket deliberately up to my head and, before I had time to take a cut at him, fired. Two dragoons of my rear rank, observing what took place, galloped up, and asked if I were hurt. And, on my laughing and shaking my head, said: 'We will punish

charge described by Hay was carried out by the 12th and 16th Light Dragoons, with the 11th Light Dragoons deployed in support but not actively engaged.

13 This French infantry was evidently from Durutte's 4eme Division, which was covering the right flank of the advancing I Corps. In *Gallantry and Discipline*, p.244, I suggested that the square was most likely that of the 85eme Ligne, which had been left out of the attack and drawn up in square to cover the flank of the French gun-line. The more recent study of events on this part of the battlefield presented in John Morewood, *Waterloo General: The Life, Letters and Mysterious Death of Major General Sir William Ponsonby 1772-1815* (Barnsley: Pen & Sword, 2016), pp.190-193, would suggest that this infantry square was in fact formed by one of the other three regiments of Durutte's command, which had moved somewhat further forward than the narrative presented in *Gallantry and Discipline* indicates. Bearing in mind that Hay uses the term 'square' indiscriminately to refer to various troop formations, including that of his own regiment, it is therefore quite possible – indeed, more likely based on accounts by other participants – that the French unit in question was in fact in heavy column rather than in square.

'Waterloo 1815' Watercolour by William Barnes-Wollen. (9th/12th Royal Lancers Museum)

the scoundrel, sir!' I had no time to say more than, 'Oh! never mind him,' when, in an instant, we were engaged, hand to hand with the Chasseurs de Cheval who were the first to encounter our advance; and, I must say, more coolness and more determined bravery was never displayed on any occasion before or since, by any set of men, than I witnessed on that trying moment of unequal strife, by our gallant left squadron of the 12th Light Dragoons.[14]

I say unequal, as our horses were much lighter than those of the enemy, and their numbers exceeded ours by three to one at least. We were for a short time so intermixed, that the fire from the infantry on our right and left, as also the showers of grape shot from their guns, was equally destructive to friend and foe.

When completely broken, having made good our charge, the colonel said to me: 'Hang it, what can detain our centre squadron I must get back and see. Lead the men out of this, and tell off the squadron behind the infantry.' These were the last

---

14   The French cavalry that counter-attacked the Left Squadron of the 12th Light Dragoons, and effectively ended its involvement in the charge, came from the 3eme Chasseurs à Cheval. Since one squadron of the French regiment had already been committed to action at an earlier stage, it would seem that it was the remaining two that intervened at this point with the odds therefore being more like two-to-one.

words, poor fellow, he uttered that day; the account he gave me of what occurred to himself I will give in its proper place.

According to his directions, I communicated with the officer commanding the squadron, and he led the remaining part of it out of action. I stopped to see the last man down the sloping and deep banks of the lane out of danger, and, for the moment, while my attention was quite absorbed in the duty, standing near the edge of the bank myself, a shell, thrown from the opposite front, burst under my horse and one of the splinters hurt his leg so severely that he sat down as a dog would do. At the moment I did not know the cause and used my spurs, but it was to no purpose, I had therefore to let myself slide over his tail; and, when trying to kick him up, some men in the hollow lane shouted, telling me to take care of myself.

On glancing round I saw two lancers coming full tilt at me, one instant more and both their lances would have been in the small of my back; one spring into the hollow deprived them of their prey, and I have little doubt that the well directed aim of some of our noble infantry of the 71st, who saw the whole transaction, accounted for them and made them pay for their temerity, by leaving their carcasses where they intended mine should be laid.[15]

No sooner had I got down into the road than several of their brave hands were held out to pull me up, amongst them a little stout sergeant, who congratulated me on my narrow escape and placed me in safety among his men.

For the two or three moments I stood with them till I recovered my horse, I had the opportunity of seeing a noble sight – which was – the Charge of the Union Brigade, as the Grays, 1st Dragoon Guards, and Enniskillen Dragoons were designated, at that moment they came down the slope a little to the right flank of the infantry, where I was standing, like a torrent, shaking the very earth, and sweeping everything before them.[16]

---

15 It is odd that Hay specifies the 71st, or Highland Light Infantry, as his rescuers as this regiment was serving on the other side of the battlefield as part of the Second Division. In that the 71st wore light infantry uniforms with trousers, and a unique cap formed by blocking up the highland bonnet into the form of a shako, it is hard to see how Hay could have mistaken any of the infantry on his part of the battlefield – be they from a highland regiment or one of the line – for that distinctive corps.

16 This reference presents a serious chronological problem with Hay's narrative, for it is generally accepted that Vandeleur ordered the 12th and 16th Light Dragoons to charge after the heavy cavalry were engaged, and in support of their attack. Although this passage from Hay's account is cited in Morewood, *Waterloo General*, p.192 to support the contention that Vandeleur's charge took place before that of the heavies, the bulk of the evidence would tend to the opposite view. Certainly, Vandeleur's brigade closed up to support the infantry at a relatively early stage in the I Corps' assault, such that Durutte's Frenchmen were able to assume a defensive stance upon the appearance of the lights and thus suffered far less by the attack of the heavies, but the descriptions of their charge – Hay's as much as those of other participants – suggest that it took place after the heavy cavalry was engaged. A number of hypotheses can be offered to explain the anomaly in Hay's timing: firstly, that, as elsewhere, his memory had become confused by the time of writing; secondly, that the Left Squadron of the 12th was attacked by the 3eme Chasseurs à Cheval whilst advancing and never took part in the main charge at all; thirdly,

Our equally brave fellows, who had done their utmost to stand against the superior weight of the French cavalry, intermixed with them and fought man to man; but the heavy brigade from their weight went over them and through them, bringing back many prisoners.

So grand a sight was perhaps never before witnessed, I know it struck me with astonishment, nor had I till then, notwithstanding my experience as a cavalry officer, ever considered what a great difference there was in the charge of a light and a heavy dragoon regiment, from the weight and power of the horses and men.

As soon as I recovered my poor horse – which was brought back to me by the man who had kindly watched his opportunity in the confusion, caused by the above mentioned charge of the Union Brigade – all covered with blood from his wounded leg, I mounted him, rather than not go on until I could get another.

I must here relate another loss I sustained besides having my favourite horse hurt – he was one of those given me by my poor father when I left home to join my regiment in Dorchester; consequently, before arriving at that distant part of the country from East Lothian, he had to travel at least seven hundred miles.

Accompanying the horses on their journey were two setters, one a particularly fine dog, which had so attached himself, from circumstances of long acquaintance, to the horse as his travelling companion, that he was almost a nuisance in the hunting-field; he would by scent trace him for miles and come up, perhaps in the middle of a run, and kiss his nose and mouth; in fact he was miserable out of his sight.

On this occasion, as I was much attached to the dog myself, I gave my servant very strict orders to secure him well with the baggage; but just as we had taken our places in the ranks before the action began, what was my dismay to find amongst the thousands assembled on the plains of Waterloo, poor Dash had discovered his master and favourite companion – his charger. Up he came in delight, jumping at the horse's head and my knee by turns, having satisfied himself at finding us out he was in raptures. With the shooting going on I dare say he fancied himself transported to a field-day on the Lammermoor Hills, where he and I had on other occasions amused ourselves with a different description of sport.

After our first charge between the French squares and our infantry – in which perilous situation he attended me – I lost sight of him, and was informed afterwards, by one of the dragoons, that he saw him killed by a shot. He was a great favourite of all the men as well as my brother officers, and was much regretted.

that what Hay saw was the continuation charge by elements of the Scots Greys against the French gun-line and not the initial charge by the whole Union Brigade.

Another error, which may safely be assumed to stem from a misread reference when the memoir was being compiled, is in Hay's account of the composition of the heavy cavalry force. The 2nd Cavalry Brigade, or Union Brigade, was composed of the 1st Royal Dragoons, 2nd Dragoons (Scots Greys), and 6th (Inniskilling) Dragoons: the 1st Dragoon Guards, which regiment Hay substitutes for the Royals, was brigaded with the Household regiments as part of the 1st Cavalry Brigade.

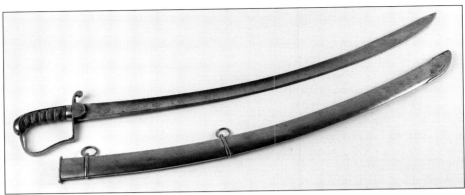

William Hay's 1796-pattern Light Cavalry Sword and scabbard, carried by him at Waterloo.
(9th/12th Royal Lancers Regimental Museum/Richard Tailby)

It was curious that another dog that had attended the troop to which I was attached, and had followed the 12th from the regiment's landing at Lisbon, in 1811, and was present in all the actions and during the several campaigns in the Peninsula, was also shot at Waterloo.

We had now – in telling off the remnants of the regiments into squadrons – an opportunity of ascertaining the severe loss we had sustained in the charge.

When we entered the field there were three squadrons, numbering fifty-four, fifty-three, and forty-eight files each. All that were left, were formed into two, one of twenty-four, the other of twenty-three files – a sad havoc indeed![17] And, excited as the feelings of all must have been at the moment, from the occurrences around us, it caused a gloom and melancholy over those who remained, not easily shaken off; nor was it lessened, when it was made known that our most gallant and much esteemed colonel was amongst them.

For my own part I never felt so much depressed in my life; nor could I, during the rest of the day, rouse my spirits, when I for a moment reflected how truly dearly that short morning's work had cost the 12th.

It may have been about 1 p.m. now, and the brigade moved a short distance further to the right flank and were drawn up by regiments, supporting artillery on the sloping ground, to the right and rear of the infantry. There we remained a

17   Casualties in the 12th Light Dragoons at Waterloo amounted to two officers, six serjeants, and 39 other ranks killed, and three officers, three serjeants, and 55 other ranks wounded for a total of 108 all ranks. Hay's figures, which imply only 94 troopers still in the saddle, plus officers and serjeants, should therefore be understood as representing the total number of men then actually present in the ranks when the regiment re-formed in the immediate aftermath of its charge: many others were unhorsed or otherwise detached, and would re-join the regiment either later in the battle or in its immediate aftermath.

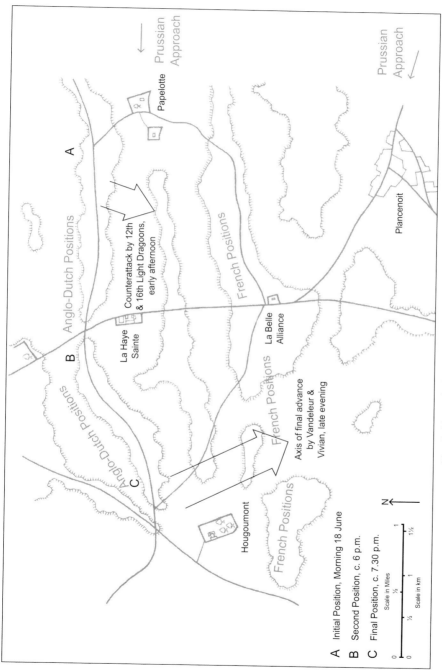

Map 3   Hay with the 12th Light Dragoons at Waterloo.

Prussian Approach

Prussian Approach

Papelotte

A

Anglo-Dutch Positions

Counterattack by 12th & 16th Light Dragoons, early afternoon

French Positions

Plancenoit

La Haye Sainte

B

La Belle Alliance

Anglo-Dutch Positions

French Positions

C

Axis of final advance by Vandeleur & Vivian, late evening

French Positions

Hougoumont

French Positions

N

A   Initial Position, Morning 18 June

B   Second Position, c. 6 p.m.

C   Final Position, c. 7.30 p.m.

0   ½   1   1½
Scale in Miles

0   ½   1
Scale in km

considerable time stationary, having a perfect view of the deadly contest going on in our front, as far as it was possible, through the clouds of smoke.

I have no language to express what I felt for the situation of our most gallant infantry, their squares had been so diminished that they appeared like little specks, surrounded by the hosts of French cavalry constantly attacking them, and standing their ground under the most murderous fire of artillery.

About two o'clock our hopes had been raised that some assistance from our allies, the Prussians, might be hourly expected, as an officer arrived with despatches for the Duke of Wellington from Marshal Blucher.

I have heard many expressed opinions on the subject of the hour at which the Prussians made their first appearance on the ground; but from the observation I myself made, I am confident their first artillery, with a detachment of cavalry, came in sight at 3.30 p.m. Their progress, it is true, was slow, the ground over which they had to march being almost impassable for their tired horses – the rain the day before, and the cutting up it had that morning, by the moving of the French Army, had made it like a sea of deep mud.

I saw their guns open fire between four and five o'clock on the French column, that seemed to me to be sent for the purpose of reconnoitring.

We changed our ground by short moves, still further to the right of the position, and every halt we made gave us a more distinct view of the struggle maintained by the infantry and artillery; it called forth admiration to observe with what cool determination these corps conducted themselves.

About 7 p.m. we had reached the extreme right flank, and the whole that remained of the British cavalry were drawn up in close column of brigades, at least, as nearly as I could understand the arrangement, our regiments were in the front line on the right flank, and, from the nature of the ground, we had a splendid view not only over our own men, but even the enemy's position. It appeared to me as if our infantry were retiring with the intention of a retreat; and as I conceived, at the time, the cavalry were placed in a situation to cover their rear, as the main road to Brussels through the forest of Soignie [sic – Forrest of Soignes] lay on our left.

The guards were drawn up on the ridge on which the cavalry stood, with their right flank to our front, behind them, and, coming in by degrees, were the different infantry divisions and brigades that fought so hard all the morning.

The artillery as it came from the same direction, from the left flank of the guards, kept changing position at a gallop. The horses looked jaded and worn out.

The whole thing, from the uncertainty to me of what was meant to be done, caused a sensation of horror at not being avenged for those friends I had lost and disappointment, after such a day's work, that we should have to leave the ground to the enemy.

But the result showed my ignorance. On the opposite side we saw nothing but moving masses of Frenchmen marching steadily on, covered by a most destructive fire from their artillery, and their cavalry on their flanks; these seemed to have been considerably thinned in their ranks – like our own.

To our right flank there seemed, to me, to be an open space over which the artillery, alongside of us, were directing a constant fire into the left flanks of the French columns as they approached; notwithstanding the deadly fire from the guns, on they came. Our infantry were in the front line lying down; and just before them, within twenty yards, was a steepish pitch, or sudden bank, in the lay of the land, deep enough to cover from sight those at the bottom from those at the top of the bank. On came the French to this bank, half their bodies and their tall, fur caps just showing over the top, when up start our guards in their front, and at the same moment the light division, which had been concealed in the corn on the flat ground on our right; and, both in front and flank, so well-directed a fire was poured in, that down the bank the Frenchmen fell, and, I may say, the battle of Waterloo was gained; and I must add that no one but an eyewitness could form an idea of the confusion and complete discomfiture of the French Army, from the well-directed and tremendous fire of the musketry poured into their ranks by our infantry in front and flank.[18]

They had been advancing in close column, cheering and seemingly so confident that the victory was their own, that the disappointment and mortification of Bonaparte must indeed have been great, as he stood on the rising ground an anxious spectator of the last great effort of his 'Invincible Imperial Guards,' who had been kept till that eventful moment disengaged.

The cavalry, as soon as the advance of the enemy was checked, moved forward at a gallop, and we actually rode over the flying masses, who had nearly all thrown down their arms, the difficulty being how to get our horses over the heaps of dying and dead.

I had seen many sights on the field after a battle, but this threw all before into complete shade. As to resistance, there was no attempt; and our men, too brave to kill disarmed men, merely rode over them, passing up to their artillery, who still continued to pour on us a heavy fire; but these we charged and took one battery after another, cutting the men down, in many instances, while employed in putting the match to the touch-hole of the gun.[19]

The 12th had somehow or other got themselves considerably in advance and rather to the right of the rest of the cavalry, when a staff-officer came from headquarters of the cavalry to caution the commanding officer that his regiment was in

18 Hay is relating the repulse of the western-most of the two attacks made by elements of the Imperial Guard against Wellington's line at the climax of the battle. This portion of the allied line was primarily defeated by the guardsmen of the 1st Brigade and the light infantry and rifles of the 3rd Brigade, the latter being the formation referred to by Hay as the light division, containing as it did the 52nd and two battalions of the 95th from the old Peninsular Light Division.
19 The 4th and 6th Cavalry Brigades took part in this advance, although the 12th Light Dragoons were relegated to a reserve role within their brigade and were not heavily engaged at this time: when Hay speaks of multiple charges, it would seem that he is either exaggerating for effect or, to take a more charitable approach, referring to the cavalry as a whole rather than to his own regiment.

danger, the right flank being quite exposed to the enemy, who were in considerable force, retiring along the ridge.

I happened to have been warned in the early part of the day to be in readiness with some picked dragoons, to undertake any particular duty that might be required; and the officer for that duty at the present time being called for, I sprang to the front calling the men I had selected before moving from our ground in the morning. But, alas! out of twenty I had chosen for their well-known steadiness and bravery, five or six only had been left to attend me on this occasion, their places were instantly supplied by others, carbines were sprung and loaded, and off I started at a sharp gallop to the top of the rising ground, when we beheld such a sight that made us look with wonder at the state into which we had thrown the gallant Army that had been contesting the ground with us all day.

Men in thousands running without arms, officers and privates struggling who should be first in the flight, some few dragoons still maintaining their arms, were all I saw of the mighty host to which we had been opposed.

I saw at a glance that these few too far outnumbered my small detachment to admit of my acting in any way but on the defensive, should it be their pleasure to attack us; I therefore satisfied myself by covering the flank of my regiment below, by extending half my men as a line of skirmishers, with the order not to provoke an encounter but be on their guard and watch patiently the retreating enemy. For about an hour I was employed in this way, when nearly all had gone out of sight.

Some of my fellows collecting together, the enemy having cleared themselves off their front, thought proper, without any orders from me, to make a dash at them and captured about a hundred prisoners. Hearing the hubbub I galloped up, rather inclined to be angry, when a French staff-officer rode from amongst them and tended me his sword, which sword I have to this day.[20]

By this time the firing from all points of the field had ceased, also the danger of being attacked, I therefore concentrated my party and dismounted the men, to wait the return of the sergeant I had sent to reconnoitre. On his return he reported that two of the men placed under his command were missing, and could give no account of them, stating that both had been posted and directed, like the others, not to move without orders. I waited till it was dark, and, my two men not arriving, I gave them up as having been killed by some chance shots that, on our arrival at the post, had been fired at us. The loss of a few men had become so common an occurrence during our avocations of the day, as to be looked upon as a matter of course.

Collecting our prisoners, I proceeded to find our regiment which had halted on the verge of the position on the left, occupied by the French the day before.

---

20 An editorial note to the original edition informed readers that the sword was then in the Royal United Service Museum, Whitehall.

I reported my return to the commanding officer, and was congratulated on its being a safe one, as when he saw us depart he never expected us to return, at least, so many of the party, therefore was agreeably surprised at the loss of only two men.[21] However, 'all is not lost that is in danger,' was a true saying in this instance.

We were a small party, talking over the events of the day, when the sergeant came up to report the two missing men had just come back, bringing with them three cuirassiers prisoners. There they stood with three as fine-looking fellows as I ever saw.

I pretended to be angry at their disobedience of my orders in leaving their post, but, on hearing the particulars, I had not a word to say in anger. My men were two Irish lads, sharp, active, brave soldiers to a fault, but both great scamps and quite up to any lark, no such words as fear or danger were in their dictionary. From the place they had been directed to stand and observe the motions of the retiring enemy, their eyes caught a glimpse of four French dragoons, going into the gateway of a farmyard.

On they went after them. On their way they met a German dragoon, him they enlisted into their service. Watching the fellows fairly into the yard, the German was posted to guard the entrance, and the two charged right into the place sword in hand; one of the Frenchman was in the act of stooping to drink, when at one cut he severed his neck; the other three immediately surrendered, to escape the same fate.

Their story was told very well, I said, but I could not believe it till I saw the dead man, which I did next morning on going to the place, and not only had ocular demonstration to satisfy me, but heard the story from the farmer himself who was a looker-on and embraced the man who did the deed, calling him his preserver and that of his family and property, as those four French stragglers had entered the yard for the purpose of plundering what he had left.

In memory of the occasion, and in justice to the two brave men, both of whom were Irish, I must mention their names – the one was Murphy the other Power – the latter, I am sorry to say, although a gallant soldier, was one of the worst characters in the whole army, but cool, determined, and brave to a fault.[22]

(I witnessed, some few months after this affair, his reception of a thousand lashes for highway robbery, and that without ever uttering a word, except desiring

---

21 The regiment was now under the command of Major Bridger, Lt. Colonel Ponsonby being missing and presumed dead after the earlier charge.

22 Private Edward Powers had been tried by Regimental Court Martial on 6 May 1815 'For irregular and unsoldierlike conduct in being drunk on the night of the 5th instant and insolent to Serjeant Bull in the execution of his duty'. Having been found guilty, he was sentenced to 300 lashes, of which he received 225 the scars of which must surely have still been painfully fresh when he fought at Waterloo. See "Register of the Non Com'd Officers, Trumpeters & Privates of the 12th Lt Dr who have been tried by a Court Martial since 1st May 1815", appended to "Confidential Report of the 12th Lt Dr 30 October 1815" by Major General Sir J.O. Vandeleur in TNA, WO27/134.

the farrier to strike him fair. On having received his punishment and being taken down, he looked round the square, formed of the brigade, and on casting his eyes to where I was posted with my troop, came across – his back lacerated and covered with blood – and requested that I would bear witness to his having on many occasions, while under my immediate command, acted as a brave soldier, and that he had that day received a punishment of a thousand lashes without complaining, which, in his idea, entitled him to a discharge.)[23]

Having satisfied myself as to the truth of the report made by the two dragoons, accounting for their absence from their post the evening before, and taking leave of the poor old Flemish farmer, whose premises were certainly in a sadly dilapidated condition from the frequent visits made to them during the operations of the previous day, I returned to my regiment and acquainted the commanding officer with all the circumstances, requesting his forgiveness for Power and Murphy.

I had scarcely seated myself to breakfast, when I received a visit from a connection and an old and intimate friend, Mr. Hay of Duns Castle, who had arrived some days before from England, for the purpose of seeing his old acquaintances of the 16th Light Dragoons, in which corps he served during the campaigns in the Peninsula, and also to introduce a young brother into the regiment, to which he was appointed as cornet.[24]

The purpose of his visit was a melancholy one. He had remained as an amateur during most part of the battle of the 18th, on different parts of the ground, occasionally coming to see the 16th; but towards evening, the business becoming too hot for him, prudence dictated the necessity of his taking leave of his brother and making his own way to the rear of the army; and his distress can better be imagined than described when, on his return to the 16th, on the morning of the 19th, Major Massey, in temporary command of the regiment, informed him his brother had been missing from nine o'clock the night before, and no account could be obtained of him either amongst the killed or wounded; the different parties sent

---

23 At this point in the original edition, a note was added as follows: 'Alison's *History of Europe*, Vol. VII., p. 203, says: § 28. "An iron discipline had given the military force a degree of firmness and regularity unknown to any other service in Europe. The use of the lash – that terrible remnant of savage rule – was still painfully frequent; and instances were not uncommon of soldiers, for inconsiderable offences, receiving five hundred, eight hundred, and even one thousand stripes – an amount of torture equal perhaps to any ever inflicted by the Inquisition." [Confirming what appears – nowadays – an incredible amount of punishment. – ED.]'

24 The elder of these two brothers was another William Hay, who had served in the Peninsula as a lieutenant in the 16th Light Dragoons from the regiment's arrival in April 1809 until he obtained his captaincy in the 60th Foot in May 1811. He had retired on half-pay in April 1812. The younger brother was Alexander Hay, who was appointed cornet in the 16th on 11 November 1813 but did not join the regiment in the field until after the conclusion of the Peninsular War and was therefore on active service for the first time during the Waterloo Campaign.

out to bury the dead had not found his body.[25] He had been last seen when the regiment was drawn up in front of a strong body of French cavalry of the guard, who were the last to retire from the field and in much too good order to admit of our weakened brigade offering them obstruction. (This body, it has been generally supposed; formed a body-guard to Napoleon, and were at no time during the battle brought into action.)[26]

But, however that may be, there they were, moving slowly at a walk, and as regularly as if marching to take up their ground for a field-day – a great contrast to the rest of the Grand Army. Having been absent myself, on an aforesaid duty, I only saw them at a considerable distance, but, was informed by my brother officers this body of cavalry, on seeing the men of our brigade approach, halted, formed line, and fired a volley – a rare thing for dragoons – and waited a few minutes, as much as to say: 'We are ready to receive your charge if you are so disposed!' and finding we did not advance, again commenced their slow retreat.

It was at this time nearly dusk, night was fast drawing on, and there may have been some little confusion attending our movements from the unexpected check to our headlong advance, but of that I cannot speak to a certainty as I was not present. Be that as it may, the first indication of some disaster having happened to young Hay, was the mare he rode coming galloping in, amongst the horses of the squadron, riderless.

A party was immediately sent back to where he had been last observed, and every means adopted by his kind friend and commanding officer, Massey, to ascertain the true cause of his, absence, but no tidings could be heard of him. His brother had come to me to tell his sad story and to ask me to accompany him in a search over the ground last occupied, while shots were still exchanged the night before.

My commanding officer immediately granted my request to do so, and we started off with one of the dragoons who stated he knew the exact spot where he was last seen; but after looking over many hundred bodies, without success, a burying party, coming to the same place, was asked the question: 'Had they seen an officer in the 16th uniform amongst the others lying on that part of the field?' A trumpeter of the regiment who formed one of the party said, the evening before, as he was returning from conducting a wounded man towards the rear, he met Cornet Hay in charge of another man going towards Waterloo, badly wounded.

On receiving this intelligence, which appeared to be, from the way it was told, quite authentic, Hay put spurs to his horse to make enquiries as directed by the trumpeter, requesting me to report what he had heard to the officers.

25 There is a confusion of names here: the officer who succeeded to the command of the 16th Light Dragoons at Waterloo was Major George Home Murray.
26 This is a reference to the *escadrons de service*, or service squadrons, drawn from the cavalry regiments of the Imperial Guard to provide Napoleon's escort.

I returned to my regiment, and about two o'clock the different parties, who had been sent either to attend the wounded or bury the dead, having come in, we commenced our march on the route towards France.

We halted that night at a small village about three leagues from the battle field, I forget its name. Next morning at daylight I received a most unpleasant order of duty, which was to retrace my steps and go to Waterloo and Brussels, taking with me an orderly dragoon, and ascertain what wounded men and horses we had at either of these places, and if any skulkers were in the rear to collect them, and bring them to their regiments.

I recollect I started on this journey with a bad grace and much out of humour, as at all times I hated being detached from my regiment to the rear; however, go I must.

The commanding officer found fault with my remonstrance, the only time I remember – during my long time as a soldier – I ever had a hard word said to me on the subject of duty. But the commanding officer, for the time during Ponsonby's absence from his honourable wounds, for some few days, at least, had been keeping up his spirits in a manner which quite put out of the question any chance of my getting justice done me, by him, on points of duty, although in other respects he was a kind-hearted man and an intimate friend and messmate of my own, therefore I made my way towards the village of Waterloo. The sights I beheld on that occasion will never be effaced from my memory.

As my orders were to go to Waterloo and Brussels, and being independent of the charge of any men, I felt at liberty to use my own discretion as to my route; the main roads being covered with the advancing army, and the country open, I rode to my right, in the direction of where our extreme left had extended, some few miles from the village of Waterloo.

My time I felt was my own, and the day before me a long one, as I started an hour before daylight; so keeping to my right hand, I soon came on to the skirts of the contested ground of the previous day.

From the loss of friends and riding alone, no companions to whom to open my thoughts, I felt far too low-spirited to encounter, what I knew must be, the dreadful sight of the field on which we had fought; therefore I bent my way towards where the great roads unite at the extreme right of the place of contest between the French cuirassiers and the English life-guards.

On my arrival there, although prepared from what I had already beheld the evening before; to witness a shocking sight, I was struck with horror at the actual masses of dead men and horses heaped together on a space of about a few hundred yards.

The day was extremely hot, and the dead bodies, already offensive, were shocking to look at. Many wounded were among them, so disabled as not to have the power to extricate themselves.

On gaining the road it was with difficulty my horse could pick his way or keep his footing as it was literally paved with steel, the cuirasses were so numerous,

'View of the village of Waterloo, the day after the Battle, June 19th 1815'. Aquatint after 'A.M.S.'
(Anne S.K. Brown Military Collection)

shining and glittering in the midday sun of June, making it quite dazzling to the
eyesight.

The ditches on each side of the road were lined with our wounded officers and
soldiers, who had been borne there to be removed in some measure from the great
thoroughfare, amongst whom I recognised several acquaintances. If I had felt sad
and in low spirits before, this did not improve my mood.

I remained some half hour offering what consolation I could to the sufferers I
knew, and contemplating with wonder the consequences of the awful struggle that
had caused such a loss of life and misery.

I proceeded on my way to Waterloo, the main road to which is a very broad one;
but it was so perfectly crammed from side to side with broken-down carriages,
waggons, baggage, men, and horses, that it was next to impossible to get along.
No expression I can use could give an idea of the confusion that prevailed on the
Brussels road on the day of which I speak: the whole baggage of the army on the
move, following up the advancing corps, besides supplies of all kinds and ammunition intermixed with hundreds of the worst and most desperate characters from
Brussels and other places, bent on plundering the dead and wounded still left on
the field of battle.

By jostling and working my way, sometimes by the sides and sometimes by the
roads, I reached the extreme end of the village of Waterloo, where I still found the

wounded in hundreds, without any covering from the strong sun, lying on every spare space of ground. There the medical men were attending, and fatigue parties commanded by officers from their different regiments; the former were quite worn out with the incessant duty they had been called upon to perform for three successive nights, and still there appeared no end to their toil. One or more I recognised, and amongst them the assistant surgeon of our own regiment. From him I made anxious enquiry respecting Colonel Ponsonby, and was gratified to hear he was still alive, and with a shadow of a hope that his wounds might not prove mortal.[27]

The first, and certainly one of the most painful visits I ever paid, was to a little wretched cottage at the end of the village, which was pointed out to me as the place where General de Lanc[e]y was lying, mortally wounded. Conceive my feelings when I state only a few months before, in December, 1814, when at my happy home, I had been in the constant habit of meeting him whilst staying with our near neighbours and intimate friends – his wife's family (the Halls) living at Dunglas.[28]

Painful as it was, it was my imperative duty to call and enquire for her and offer my poor services.

How wholly shocked I was, on entering, to find her seated on the only broken chair the hovel contained by the side of her dying husband!

An amiable, kind, and beautiful young woman, I had so recently left in the midst of her own delightful family, surrounded by every luxury, at that most trying moment in want of every comfort, and plunged in the deepest distress.

I made myself known, she grasped me by the hand, and pointed to poor De Lanc[e]y, covered with his coat, with just a spark of life left. Offering consolation would have been an insult and hypocrisy at such a moment; but imagine to yourself the kind-hearted and high-minded young woman, in the midst of her own deep affliction, looking earnestly in my face, pale from long fatigue, and covered with dust from my already long ride in the heat, she rose, and beckoned me out of the room as if she thought it too much for me; and, returning herself, brought me some wine in an old broken teacup – the only article of the description in the house. I bade her farewell and proceeded some little distance farther into the village, where I had pointed out to me the house in which Colonel Ponsonby lay.

The medical officer met me at the door, said I might see the colonel for a few minutes, that he had some faint hopes of his recovery, but it all depended on the turn the wounds might take within the next forty-eight hours. Preceded by the doctor, I went into a comfortable room; he was quite sensible and delighted to see me. The doctor left us alone, and he told me he must not speak for fear of causing

---

27 The badly-wounded Ponsonby famously survived a lengthy ordeal on the battlefield before being recovered on the morning of the 19th and taken for treatment.

28 Colonel Sir William De Lancey, Deputy Quartermaster General, was mortally wounded by a cannonball at Waterloo and died ten days later, famously and tragically nursed by the wife he had married only a little over two months previously.

the wounds in his lung to bleed afresh; but requested me to relate every particular to him as well as I could, after he parted from me on making the charge.

Having done this I took my leave by order of the doctor. I next went to see, at a house opposite, Colonel Hay of the 16th, who was also very badly wounded. His medical man immediately told me there was not the slightest hope of his recovery, that he was free from pain, and I might go in and see him. I found him propped up with pillows in his bed, quite light-hearted, happy, and truly like a soldier, perfectly prepared to die. He conversed on the subject of the action as coolly as a man untouched and said he was quite aware the nature of his wounds was such as to deprive him of any chance of life; asked about all his friends, and how his regiment had conducted itself after he fell; and lastly, that he was particularly glad to see me, as he had not left a will, and although he had not much to leave, still the little he had he wished his brother to find out where it was; he related to me all the particulars and directions he wished to give, and then took, as he considered, his last kind and affectionate leave of me. But, I am truly happy to say, both he and his doctor were far out in their calculations, as, instead of dying, he recovered rapidly, and is alive and well and a General officer this day. Long may he continue to enjoy all happiness![29]

Having ascertained all I required on points of duty, both on the service I was engaged upon and also as a friend to those suffering in the village of Waterloo, I was nearly worn out by long and continued fatigue, and I sought but in vain for a resting-place, as every description of building was full to overflowing with those much better entitled, from their bodily suffering, than myself, to what accommodation the place offered; consequently, as soon as my horse had been fed and sufficiently rested, I proceeded on my way to Brussels.

I anxiously kept a lookout, as I went along, at the numerous baggage trains, to discover that belonging to the 12th, that I might indulge in a change of clothes, those I was wearing, bad at first starting, as already stated, had been on my back for five days, which had not improved them.

At last I descried the regimental baggage, but conceive my consternation and horror when informed that my own had been plundered, and my horses and every article I possessed stolen by the rascally Belgians who had left the field of battle, deserting their ranks, for the sake of plundering and murdering their allies on the highway, taking advantage of the confusion that existed. Many other officers suffered in the same way as myself, I had only to make up my mind that what could not be cured must be endured, and continued on my way sorrowing.

29 Lt. Colonel James Hay was a long-serving officer who had risen through the ranks of the 16th Light Dragoons during the Peninsular War by the end of which he was commanding the regiment. His wounds at Waterloo are recorded as being so severe that he could not be moved from the battlefield for eight days (Dalton, *Waterloo Roll Call*, p.87) which does place a question mark over William Hay's timings here. James Hay eventually made a full recovery, and died in 1854 with the rank of lieutenant general.

On my arrival at Brussels, I was much struck by the difference in the appearance presented by the streets to what they were on my former visit to that city: the shops were all closed – fewer persons were to be seen – soldiers, in all the different uniforms of the Armies, limping about or assisting each other to places of refuge.

My first duty was to report myself to the officer in command, General Adams [sic].[30] On reaching his quarters and sending in my name, I was instantly admitted and received by the poor general, who, although in command was lying wounded, in bed; I had the honour of his acquaintance previously, and was met by that most gentlemanly officer as a friend. In the same house was another acquaintance, his *aide-de-camp* – Colonel Blair – also wounded.[31] From them I went to visit an old and valued friend, the late Hon. V. Stuart, whom I had heard was badly wounded, I had the melancholy satisfaction of sitting at his bedside in conversation with him till the surgeons arrived to amputate, which sight I could not bear.[32]

The only officer of my own corps was Captain Sands, who had reached Brussels very badly wounded, he commanded the centre squadron at our first charge on the 18th.[33] On going to his house I found him in much suffering from wounds in the body; he complained bitterly of not receiving attention from any medical man, and requested me to endeavour to procure one to come and see him. For this purpose I immediately proceeded to a large convent, at which place I was told I should find the head of the medical staff. On my arrival, my feelings were put to a more severe test than any expression of mine can give an adequate description of.

The long passages, corridors, yards, and every space of ground in and about the place, was covered with wounded soldiers, lying, sitting, or reclining; I had to pass through them to get to the officer, to whom I had to make my application. I found him in a long, broad room, with a table down the centre on which were lying some twenty or thirty poor fellows, under the operation of the doctors' knives.

Seeing suffering on the field of battle, where all are alike exposed and actively engaged, is nothing compared with this, which made me feel quite sick. However, stern duty to my poor brother officer demanded my determination to execute the commission I went there to perform; I therefore waited for the young practitioner, to whom I had been introduced, while he finished amputating the leg of a poor

---

30   Major General Frederick Adam – not Adams – had commanded the 3rd Brigade at Waterloo where the role of his command in turning back the last French attack has already been noted. He had previously served in Eastern Spain.

31   This officer was not in fact Adam's aide but, rather, the brigade-major of the 3rd Brigade, Major Thomas Hunter-Blair of the 91st Highlanders. Hunter-Blair received a brevet promotion to lieutenant colonel for his services at Waterloo, but he was not 'Colonel Blair' when Hay encountered him.

32   This would seem to be in fact Colonel the Hon. William Stuart, the 'V' no doubt being a typographical error. Stuart was Third Major of the 1st Foot Guards and commanded the 3rd Battalion of that regiment in the Waterloo campaign during the course of which he received a serious wound to the left arm that required the amputation which Hay could not bear to watch.

33   Captain Edwin W.T. Sandys – the surname is pronounced the way Hay spells it, so this one error that can readily be forgiven – was a veteran officer of long service with the 12th Light Dragoons.

fellow, fearing to lose sight of him, and knowing full well how many calls for assistance each had to meet, I remained till his business was over.

Accompanied by him I returned to poor Sands, who said, on my going into his room: 'Oh! I am so sorry I gave you the trouble, I feel much better, all the pain has left me, I suffer only from coldness in my feet.' I retired to let the doctor look at his wound, who, after a few minutes, followed me, saying: 'I regret to say your friend cannot live many hours, mortification has set in, and his sufferings will soon be at an end.' His words were only too true, at 8 p.m. he breathed his last.

The fatigue and the sights I had already seen made me feel quite overcome and unequal to further duty that night, with difficulty I got myself put up in a small room in one of the hotels.

I employed myself next day visiting the different hospitals and houses where the men were – for almost every private house had been converted into a receptacle for the wounded soldiers – and, to their everlasting credit, I found not only the whole of the rooms in the houses of the best families occupied by the men of the British Army, but the ladies of the houses attending and dressing their wounds, and nursing them like their own children.

I found in some houses one portion of the family attending to the sick, and the others making lint, while the gentlemen of the families were out in the roads and streets collecting those who required aid, and conducting them to their houses. Many families whom I knew had taken coaches to the field of battle, taking cooling drinks to administer and bandages for wounds, returning to the city with two or three soldiers who were taken to their houses to be nursed; indeed, I can firmly assert from personal knowledge, too great praise cannot be bestowed on the citizens of Brussels, for their great attention and kindness on that occasion.

Towards the afternoon of the 21st, having performed the duties for which I had been sent, I was proceeding to the quarter-master-general's quarters, to procure a route for my return to re-join my regiment, when, at a distance, riding along the main street, I observed Mr. Hay; upon asking about his brother, he told me all the information we had received from the trumpeter had proved incorrect, that he had ever since been enquiring without success, and intended next day to start for the headquarters of the army, with a view of getting an application made to the commander-in-chief of the French troops to ascertain, if possible, if his brother had been carried away prisoner.

We dined together, and, as my duties were finished, it was agreed we would leave Brussels in company next morning, take Waterloo and the field of battle on our way, with a view of making further search.

I started on the 22nd, my party having increased by the addition of my servant, a sergeant, and two or three dragoons I found at Brussels, who had been detached there on duty. Much to the credit of my regiment, there was not a single man belonging to it in the rear who had not been wounded.

On reaching Waterloo I found all my suffering surviving friends better, and hopes entertained of ultimate recovery – but many had died! We reached the field about noon; the weather was hot almost beyond endurance, and the smell arising from the carcasses insufferable, it was not my first visit to a place of the kind, but the business I was now called upon to perform required a much more minute survey of the work of destruction.

Countless numbers of men lay stretched in death, and amongst them some thousands of wounded still unattended. Groups of peasants were parading all over the plain in search of plunder. Most of the bodies were stripped. It was a sight I cannot, even at this distance of time, let my mind rest on without horror.

Amongst those heaps of dead we looked in vain to find poor Alexander Hay, turning them over and examining minutely one after another all about the place where he had been last seen. On the ground were several patrols of Prussians shooting their own and the French wounded soldiers, who were beyond recovery.

Although it seemed a piece of barbarity at the time, I am sure it was a great act of charity, as their sufferings must have been truly awful, with the heat and lack of anything to quench their thirst for three days under a scorching sun; in fact many begged us to put them out of their misery.

After continuing our melancholy and most unpleasant task for some three hours, we gave it up as hopeless and left the scene of distress to proceed on our forward march.

The main roads were still choked with moving masses of every description, which impeded our progress to such a degree, had we followed in the line, as to make it tedious beyond bearing; but, William Hay being anxious to lose as little time as possible, I proposed we should take a line for ourselves direct through fields and forests, by country roads, leading towards the great road, which we should strike at a certain point, two or three days' journey from where we then were. Our maps were consulted and we took our line accordingly; our wish was to head the infantry columns, as soon as possible, and make up to the cavalry which were in advance.

Towards evening we found ourselves in the midst of a large forest, quite out of the lead of the army, and both ourselves and horses much fatigued. We had some provisions with us, therefore agreed to call a halt for the night, when one of the dragoons, whom I was in the habit of sending to keep a look-out on our flank, mentioned that at a short distance he had observed a farmhouse. To this it was agreed we should bend our steps.

As we neared the place pointed out, we came in sight of a large, neat house in the Flemish style of building, with spacious stabling, seemingly well supplied with hay and straw stacks. On our arrival at the door we found the house already occupied, and piles of baggage inside and about the doorway.

From the appearance of the men about the yard, we took them for the followers of some of our German or Prussian Allies, and, on questioning a woman at the door, she informed us it was the baggage of an officer who had ordered the rooms to be got ready and was expected by his servants every minute, and all the stabling was already occupied by his horses; but that half a mile distant we should find another large farm where there was no one. To this we bent our way.

We were well received, got ourselves and horses put up, something to eat was provided, and we found ourselves comfortable enough; our only want was some cigars, which neither of us had; but, having observed at the first house one of the men, whom we took for Germans, smoking, we despatched a servant to try and procure some from our neighbours. In a short time our messenger returned, but without the cigars, and with the news that the whole party had decamped in great haste soon after our departure. On going to the place to make further enquiry, conceive our disappointment when we ascertained that the party we took for Germans were none other than the servants, horses, and baggage of a French general officer, stealing their way through the byways into France, who, fearing to remain so near us, thought it prudent to beat a retreat under cover of the night, which had now set in. We, being quite strangers to the roads and whereabouts, were prevented from following to make a capture, which, I must confess, I was much inclined to do at all hazards, but my companions overruled me. I regretted losing such a prize, particularly at a moment when I was in the greatest need, of everything.

We pursued our way in the morning, and for several days had to march and put up with great inconvenience and discomfort. Our provisions ran out both for ourselves and horses, and, as every town and village we came to was deserted by the inhabitants and fully occupied by the advancing troops, we could get nothing for love or money. One day we were so hard pressed as to have to beg a bit of bread from the servant of a general officer, who, am sure, if he had known of our distress, would have made us welcome partakers of what fare he had for himself, as a kinder friend, better man, or more gallant officer did not exist in the whole British Army. Before and since I have had the honour to account him not only an acquaintance, but a sincere benefactor; but my modesty would not admit of my making myself known at the time by intruding on him. (I speak of General Sir T. P.)[34]

About the eighth day after leaving Brussels, I was rejoiced at making up to my own regiment, and joined it, taking leave of my friend, who proceeded to Lord Wellington's quarters. Our first halting-place was at a town called Quevauville, some thirty miles from Paris, where it became necessary to recruit our horses, who had been on constant long marches ever since the 15th.[35]

---

34   It is not clear which general officer is here meant. Sir Thomas Picton was killed at Waterloo, and no other 'Sir T.P.' figured amongst Wellington's subordinate commanders in this campaign. If the 'T' is assumed to be a typographic error, then possibly the reference is to Sir Denis Pack; another option, if it is the 'P' that is erroneous, would be Sir Thomas Bradford. Since Bradford would have been on his way to join the army, having arrived in the theatre after Waterloo, whereas Pack would have been with his brigade, he seems the more likely of the two possibilities for Hay to have encountered whilst still in the rear of the advance.

35   The location would seem to be Quevauvillers, which is, however, near Amiens and at a greater distance from Paris than thirty miles but which otherwise fits with Hay's chronology and the movements of the allied armies.

The Prussians had been in the town or skirted it before our arrival; consequently, all the inhabitants had left their houses and contents at the mercy of the conquerors. Our Prussian allies had helped themselves to all that had been left worth taking, and the town, a considerable one, with many respectable dwellings in it, was quite destitute; forage for the horses was very scarce, and nothing to be had in the shape of provisions for ourselves.

As it was expected our stay might be extended to some time, as negotiations were, we understood, on foot for the evacuation of Paris, it was deemed requisite to send foraging parties, as a protection, to accompany the commissaries in search of forage, as the Prussian irregulars would not have been over scrupulous about hanging any individual who interfered with their prerogative of plunder, and keeping to themselves what had come in their way.

Amongst other officers, I was detached with a party on this duty, and proceeded for some ten or twelve miles from the main track of the army to a village in which, from information the commissary had received, we were likely to obtain everything in the shape of forage, and also rations for the men – no troops having been in that direction up to them.

On our arrival we saw several large houses and many small ones, a good church, but not an inhabitant or living soul to be seen, even the wine shops seemed deserted; we looked round in every direction for some individual from whom to make enquiry which was the mayor's or principal man of the place's house, but in vain. After a little consultation, it was agreed we should try to open one of the great gates leading into a goodly looking mansion surrounded by high walls.

I knew that it behoved me to act with great caution, orders from the duke having been given warning all parties on the subject of doing anything likely to offend the people of the country, or plundering; therefore, before attempting to use force, every method was tried to ascertain if any living beings were within the walls, but, after knocking and battering to no purpose, one of my men got on the top of the wall and exclaimed: 'Oh! what a fine place! the yard is full of poultry, cows, sheep, and forage of every kind.'

After such a report, to raise the siege would have been madness; on questioning him further, he said the house seemed all shut up, still there was one window which appeared sufficiently open to allow whoever was within to observe any movement on the outside, and that he strongly suspected there were people concealing themselves.

We, therefore, made renewed efforts to effect an opening, but still without success. The wall on the inside was much too high for the dragoon on the top to get down without the chance of hurting himself, and the gate much too strong to break down. It occurred to me, a pistol shot directed to the front door might have the desired effect of disturbing the inmates, if there were any in the house; I, therefore desired him to load and fire.

No sooner was the report of the pistol heard in the interior of the house, than out of the half-window, seen open, was thrust the long yellow visage of an elderly

Frenchman, his head covered with a red night-cap, calling out for mercy, and enquiring whether we were English or Prussian soldiers.

He seemed, after he had got an answer, to doubt the truth; however, finding further resistance of no use, he capitulated, opening the great gates.

On entering we found we had been in no way deceived by the soldier's report, as the garrison was well provided indeed, with everything, not only to feed a hungry regiment, but with comforts of all kinds.

The old man immediately expressed his delight at seeing the English troops, in whom he placed every confidence, and commenced again to barricade his doors. He then told us he himself was the mayor of the place, that the whole country round was living in dread of a visit from the Prussian soldiers, but that he was ready and willing to assist our commissary in every way in obtaining the rations and forage he was searching for; and, on being told he would receive immediate payment for every article, he was not only astonished, but overjoyed at his good luck.

Orders were immediately given for his family to come forth from their hiding-places, wine was brought out for the men, and we were made welcome visitors.

He considered he had got sufficient protection, and urgently requested me to remain with my party and make his house my quarters, offering, on the part of his family, everything I could want to render us all comfortable. On telling him I must obtain first my commanding officer's leave to that effect, he at once, French-like, proposed a bribe. I told him that if he would make up a basket of good things and wine of the best, including champagne, for Monsieur le Commandant, I would see what could be done.

The commissary, having completed his requisitions and received orders from the mayor, in his official capacity, for the delivery of forage, rations, etc., from the different farmers in the neighbourhood, for the troops quartered in the town of Quevauville, took his departure accompanied by a bullock-cart loaded with many good things, as an offering, most acceptable in the opinion not only of our host, but also of myself, knowing as I did the tastes of our old commander (the late Colonel Bridger) for the good things of this life.

With this cart I sent, as an escort, a dragoon, with a note from me expressing the wish of the mayor that my small party should remain quartered on him, not only as a protection, but to enable him to fulfil his duty by sending daily supplies for the use of the regiment. As I expected, the orderly returned with a message fully acquiescing in my recommendation and the views of the mayor; I, therefore, prepared to settle myself in, certainly, most comfortable quarters for the time being. Not only necessaries were most readily supplied to myself and the men, but luxuries of every kind were pressed upon us.

The females of the family had gained confidence and joined the party at dinner; these consisted of madame and her two very pretty daughters; the mayor; himself a perfect *bon vivant* of the old French school, always produced a first-rate well-cooked dinner and most excellent wine of almost every description.

I discovered, in conversation, that the dread of the inhabitants was very great and that the lower orders had betaken themselves with their movables into the church, as a place of safety, barricading the doors; others had retired into neighbouring woods; and some had followed the example of our host, and shut themselves within their own high walls.

At this place, and enjoying the good things as described, and the rest we so much needed, we remained about three days unmolested, when, one morning, a loud knocking was heard at the gate. The old man came to me, with consternation pictured in his face, to say a party of Cossacks were drawn up in front, and requested my interference.[36] He then took me to a place I had not discovered before where, through a sort of loop-hole, one could command a view of all that was going on outside the walls without being observed.

I found on reconnoitring there was a party of ten or twelve, as ill-looking and dirty a set of fellows as the world could produce, in front of the gate; I told him I must open the gate to speak to the newcomers, but this he strongly objected to, declaring that when once the fellows saw what was within, we should not be able to get the gates shut again on them.

However, I took my own plan, greatly against his wish, and, after a little gentle remonstrance and telling the man, who appeared to be their leader, that the village was under the special protection of the English troops, I found him very civil; and he, to the great delight of the inmates, immediately withdrew his men.

On my return from the parley, I found the plate and all valuables, which had been previously displayed for the honour of our visit, had disappeared into their hiding-places, and even the ladies' dresses had been changed for others much commoner.

The storm blew over for a time and the old gentleman and I continued our interrupted smoke, reflecting on the recent disturbance. I was wicked enough to enjoy what had passed as a good joke at my landlord's expense of fright – not so with him, he reflected deeply what might still be the consequences of his unscrupulous visitors giving information, to other parties, of the good things my imprudence had displayed to their sight, by opening the gates.

I began to be a little apprehensive myself, from the reports occasionally brought me by the men, who, having discovered the loop-hole in the wall, obtained from it news of frequent stragglers evidently on the look-out, which gave me a sort of uneasiness, as I feared that a camp of Cossacks could not be far distant, and I well knew there was no trusting these gentlemen when plunder came in their way.

---

36   As is made plain as the narrative progresses, Hay is using 'Cossacks' to describe Prussian cavalry. Since he later also terms them irregulars, it is to be inferred that these men likely came from one of the volunteer jäger detachments still attached to several Prussian regular regiments as a hold-over from the campaigns of 1813-14. Alternatively, these may have been men from one of the mounted Landwehr regiments.

True, the battle of Waterloo had made them feel very friendly towards the English, and, I must say, to do those of the irregular Prussians justice, who came in contact with myself, that if a wish were expressed it was immediately complied with; but I was well aware of the many and dreadful injuries which had been received by them in their own country and family circles from the French troops, which justly excited their great desire for vengeance, now that they had it in their power to pay off old scores.

That night I kept my small party on the alert, and when a knocking came at the gate – which occurrence became more frequent – the answer was given from the loop-hole by a man stationed there, that these were English officers' quarters – which had the desired effect.

However, next forenoon brought its miseries, as an orderly arrived to say the regiment had received a route to proceed on their march, and directing me to join forthwith. On hearing the news, I thought the poor old Frenchman would have gone out of his mind; he offered half of what he possessed in the world for me to remain as his protector.

To make matters worse, just at this time, a strong body of Cossacks, commanded by an officer of rank, drew up in front of the house; the usual knocking commenced.

By this time our horses had been bridled, and the dragoons ready to mount for starting. To save my poor old friend, as far as lay in my power, I thought I would use a little stratagem; consequently, sore against his inclination, I ordered the gates to be thrown open.

Drawing my party across the opening, I went out and demanded, in French, what officer commanded the new arrival, requesting to speak to him. On this a young and gentlemanly man rode forward, and saluted me. I found he spoke French perfectly. I invited him to come within the yard, told him the house, its inmates and all it contained were placed under my protection for services rendered the English troops by the master, who was mayor; at the same moment introducing the old gentleman, who by this time had again assumed the red night-cap, standing looking the picture of wonder and dismay at what I was doing.

My plan had the desired effect of his offering to immediately withdraw his troops, leaving the house under the protection of their English Allies; but that was not my drift. I then said I should take advantage of a highly honourable man as himself, looking for quarters, to give them up to him and withdraw our men, feeling aware, from the recommendation I had given, all the property, I was there to protect, would be in equally good hands.

The compliment took, to the delight of the mayor, and a bottle of the best champagne was immediately ordered, to drink the health of his new friend, and *bon voyage* to his late protector.

During the short time it took to discuss our 'Stirrup cup,' I entered into conversation with the Prussian officer – a soldier-like and manly fellow. He expressed great admiration of the English character and their gallant deeds at Waterloo, and, at the same time, his greatest detestation and hatred of the French. He said:

'Fortunately, you, as a country, have never been subject to their diabolical proceedings, cruelty, and oppression.' Then he related to me a portion of his family history, begging I would judge for myself whether, if placed in his situation, my feelings and wish for revenge, would not be equally as strong as his.

The names of the places I forget, but he stated to me this: His family, at the time the French army invaded Prussia, consisted of his father – a man of considerable property and who farmed his own land – his mother, seven sons, and one daughter. Looking round the yard and at the house of the mayor, he said his father's home was of the same description but larger, well-stocked with everything, as that was. On the morning when the French troops entered their village, his father and five brothers had been called on to take arms, and join in the defence of their country.

He, with his elder brother about twelve years of age; his mother who at the time was very ill in bed; and his sister, a girl of about fifteen, were the only inmates of the house, when a French officer with a party of soldiers arrived. The door was immediately broken open, the soldiers commencing the work of plunder. His brother, who either refused to tell or did not know where something they asked for was, was shot like a dog. From his own youth he supposed he escaped their notice, and so took an opportunity to conceal himself; but his sister, alas! was forced away by the brutes, and never afterwards heard of.

While his men were in the act of plundering, the officer had made his way from room to room in the house, calling on the old woman, acting as a servant, to conduct him to her mistress. He was informed she was in bed and too ill to see him, but offered everything the house contained to be placed at his service. Even that did not satisfy the savage! He broke into the room where the poor mother lay near her confinement, and commanded her to get up and conduct him to where the money was hidden.

She pleaded her condition, and told him where he would find everything they possessed in the shape of valuables, but not satisfied, and finding her unable to get out of bed, he stripped her of the covering and ran his sword through her body and that of the infant, to which she was on the point of giving birth.

Having related to me the foregoing, he asked: would not my feelings under the same circumstances have caused me to swear eternal hatred to the French race. Except himself, his own family were extinct; his father and brothers had all been killed, and he was alone left to avenge their death.

He also added that before the demons left the house a firebrand was applied by order of the same officer, and what had been, till then, known as a happy and comfortable home, was left a desolate blackened waste.

Under cover of the night, he managed to reach the lines of the Prussian Army, and attached himself first as a camp follower, to a party of independent Cossacks, some of whom knew his family and took care of him. As soon as he was able to carry a lance he was attached to the corps, and for his conduct had been promoted by degrees to the rank he now held – that of captain of a squadron.

He assured me, notwithstanding what he had told me and his own determination to avenge himself, he would respect the wish I had expressed to spare and protect the house and family I had given into his care, and when he left the place he would give an order for others to do the same. He again expressed himself proud of the alliance and confidence of his brave English friends. I took my leave on this assurance, and made the best of my way to overtake my regiment, which had, by this time, gained a considerable distance on their way towards the capital of France.

At the time I overtook them they were encamped on the skirts of a village about eight miles from Paris;[37] there we halted all night, uncertain what was to be the event of the next day, as news kept constantly arriving from the front that the Prussians, under Blucher, were hotly engaged, and it was expected the French army would concentrate for another battle.

Next morning, before daybreak, we again commenced our march, but very slowly and with many halts. When the sun rose to its height, Montmartre, the high grounds, and even parts of Paris itself, were to be seen.

Our brigade now formed the advance-guard of the army moving on the road; the enemy's cavalry kept falling back as we advanced, and frequent halts for flags of truce took place. Whenever their rear-guard came to a halt our light artillery were ordered to the front, so on we crept till, towards the afternoon, we reached the village of Neuilly. Passing through it, we kept the left bank of the river Seine for some ten miles, when we came to a halt in readiness to cross at a moment's notice in support of the Prussians, who had been hotly engaged all day, and had, by this time of the evening, driven the French troops from all their strong grounds to the very walls of Paris.

We remained during the night in readiness for any movement where our services might be required to support our allies, or take part with them as needed by circumstances. In the morning we were first informed negotiations had been opened for the surrender of Paris and the retiring of the French troops.

By this time a great part of our army had arrived and taken up a position on the side of Montmartre, at which point also the enemy's posts had been driven in. During the day our brigade kept slowly retracing their steps towards Neuilly, and towards evening encamped in the gardens and splendid grounds of the Minister of Marine, some two miles from the above-named village.[38]

The house, a large one, fitted up in a style of grandeur equal to any palace, was occupied as a barrack, and totally ransacked from cellar to garret; the grounds

---

37   A letter from Lieutenant Vandeleur, dated 1 July 1815, places the regiment at Roissy-en-France, fifteen miles northeast of the centre of Paris, and today the site of the Charles de Gaulle Airport. See Bamford (ed.) *With Wellington's Outposts*, p.154.

38   This would be Neuilly-sur-Seine, which was then to the north-west of Paris but has now been absorbed by it, and is not to be confused with Neuilly-sur-Marne to the east of the city. The Minister of Marine at this time was Denis Decrès, who had also served Napoleon in that capacity 1801-1814.

'Cavalry on the March' Anonymous ink sketch. (Anne S.K. Brown Military Collection)

were laid waste, I must say, in rather a wanton manner, but we thought it all fair to punish the treachery of those who had again attached themselves as followers of Napoleon – and the owner of the house was one of these.

In the grounds was a large sheet of water, and on it was anchored a beautiful model of a small ship-of-war, complete in every way; her name was the *Roi de Russie*. She was large enough to contain a considerable party of pleasure seekers. Some of the dragoons stripped off their clothes, swam out to the ship, hoisted all her flags to the mast-head – the French tricolour below the British ensign, at the top – fired a salute from the guns on board, placed on her what combustibles they could collect, cut her adrift, and set them on fire; and, I must say, we enjoyed the mischief of seeing the French ship burn to the water's edge.

Next day we again retired, passed through Neuilly, and took up a camping ground about a mile from the entrance into the village where the corps of the army, to which our brigade was attached, were now concentrating. I was ordered to take thirty men with me, to return to the front and to report myself and party to the field officer in command of the outlying pickets that were established in the village of Neuilly close to the left end of the bridge, of that name, over the Seine.

I was glad to find the officer under whose orders I was to act, was the man of all others (from past experience, having had the honour of being under his immediate command in the 52nd), for whose judgment, gallantry, and conduct I had the greatest possible respect, and for whom I felt a strong personal regard, the present

General Lord Seton – at that time Lieutenant-Colonel Colbourne [sic].[39] He conde-scendingly left it to my own judgment how to dispose of my party and place them out of sight, under cover, with the exception of the vedettes. I was truly delighted to find myself acting on this duty in concert with all my old friends and acquaint-ances of the light dragoons.

On the opposite, or Paris, end of the bridge was a strong body of French troops with their sentries; on that side were double abattis dividing ours from theirs and the bridge itself mined, and which point was looked upon by both parties as neutral ground.

We remained inactive all the forenoon, but towards evening a strong body of French cavalry, perhaps fifteen hundred men, marched down and posted them-selves on each side of the road leading to Paris.

We looked at each other for some time at a distance, at last the restless disposi-tion of the French, tinctured at the time with an inclination to have some talk over past events, inclined the officer in command of the cavalry to send a flag of truce to demand permission to water his horses in the Seine. On its arrival at the first abatti on their side, I went with Lord Seton to meet them across the second on our side; of course the request was complied with.

While so large a body of horses were watering, which took a considerable time, as all the nonsense of a covering party in readiness in case of attack was kept up and our pickets under arms, etc,, etc., gave an excellent opportunity for the officers of both sides to meet and converse on neutral ground, which levee was attended by several officers from each army.

All went on in a most friendly way, wine and brandy were sent for, to drink to each other, when a scene took place which so disgusted the better and more gentlemanly feelings of the English officers present, that we dispersed with not a very good opinion of the dignity and high bearing of the certainly handsome and soldier-like officer who commanded the French dragoons.

Curiosity had induced some civilians to scramble over the abattis for the purpose of having a better view, I suppose, of their unwelcome visitors – the English soldiers. Amongst them was a little old French gentleman, dressed in the fashion of centuries back: his long cane, with a gold head, in his hand, dun-coloured socks and buckled shoes on his feet, queue behind his head, and a white poodle dog at his side; such is the picture of the character to which I allude.

In a most inoffensive way the old gentleman moved forward, nearer to where we stood, the better to gratify his sight, when a French officer, like a tiger cat, sprang

---

39   Hay manages to get wrong both the current and future names of this officer, the famous Sir John Colborne of the 52nd Light Infantry, who was later created Lord Seaton and who was at this time deputising for the wounded Adam as commander of the 3rd Brigade. Hay could not have been 'under his immediate command' prior to this point, as Colborne was not appointed to the 52nd until after Hay had left the regiment.

from amongst us, caught the old man by his long tail, and gave him a sound horse-whipping, swearing at him for having intruded into their company as a listener!

At this conduct we all felt so shocked that we spontaneously broke away, and retired across to our side of the bridge, leaving the French officers to judge from our precipitate retreat what we thought of the conduct of their commanding officer.

Towards evening an order came to Lord Seton that, by the terms of the treaty signed by the commission sitting on the negotiations for the capitulation of Paris, he was to take possession of the bridge, and advance the outposts to the distance of half a mile on the Paris road.

I accompanied his lordship, with a flag of truce in our turn, and we were met by the same officer who committed the assault on the old man.

On Lord Seton intimating to him the order he had received, the reply made was that his orders were to maintain and defend his ground, which he was determined to do, let the consequences be what they may.

I shall never forget, as long as I live, the cool soldier-like demeanour of that truly gallant officer, Lord Seton, as he answered the Gascon bully, who pointed out the large body of French troops, drawn out in column, declaring their determination to defend the bridge and road to the last man, rather than retire an inch. 'Very well, I will allow you fifteen minutes' (taking out his watch) 'to consider your determination, and' – pointing to where our army lay in camp – 'there lies our support, the first shot that is fired will put them all in motion.'

Opposed to us may have been some eight or ten thousand French troops, and I do not think our pickets consisted of more than two thousand men, and my small party were all the dragoons. However, having expressed his determination, we retired to wait the expiration of the time allowed. Meanwhile the troops assembled on their alarm grounds, pickets stood to arms, and my dragoons were directed to show themselves only sufficiently to denote we had cavalry, without displaying how few in number.

All was in readiness, the prescribed time had expired, the bugles of the Rifle Brigade (or, at that time, the old 95th) struck up, and the light division were in motion to take their chance against any numbers. In a few seconds the abattis were in possession of a body of skirmishers, ready to resist any attack; while a party had piled their arms and were directed to clear away all obstruction under cover of their fire, if necessary.

However, the determined and bold step of our gallant leader had the desired effect: the Commanding officer of the French ordering the retreat of his troops; as they retired, we slowly advanced till we occupied the ground denoted by the orders. There our pickets were again posted, and we remained for the night quiet and in full possession of the leading road, within three miles of the capital of France.

The picket under my orders were some quarter of a mile furthest in advance, the infantry occupying the houses and sides of the road in my rear. One of the greatest difficulties I had to contend against all night was keeping my men, when on vedette, sober.

The French vedettes, who were posted about two hundred yards in front of ours, galloping up to them, when unobserved by their officers or myself, and, placing their horses alongside, pulled out bottles of brandy, and insisted on drinking together – a great temptation to resist truly.

It was to me so new a sight, that, although angry, I could not help laughing when it was first reported to me by the sergeant on patrol duty; nor could I believe what he said, till I had witnessed it myself.

When I spoke to the French dragoons on the impropriety of their conduct, and told them that, if insisted on, I must make them prisoners, they expressed their willingness to be sent to the rear if I would allow them the sum their horses would sell for. When I told them, in good-humour, that prisoners could not dictate terms after being taken, they offered to desert if we would take them to the rear, which some forty or fifty actually did, during the night.

At daybreak I was directed to advance my picket and post them in a large enclosed garden a short distance from the triumphal arch opposite, to an *auberge*, where the committee of negotiation was sitting. I should have been relieved that morning by another officer and party but that did not take place.

Although annoyed at the time at the seeming neglect of the adjutant, I soon became reconciled to my fate and enjoyed my extra day's duty very much. As I mentioned before, some forty or fifty dragoons of different regiments had presented themselves as deserters, and others still kept coming, and, as they came in, I brought them into the enclosure which kept them quite out of sight. Their motive for desertion was soon very evident: it was to get off marching with their regiments, which by this time were understood to intend to evacuate Paris that evening. There was also the temptation of selling their horses and appointments, which indulgence was generally granted to deserters from the enemy.

The infantry officers on picket, with whom I had breakfasted in company at the *auberge*, having heard of my depôt of French horses, conceived they might mount themselves at a cheap rate, and resorted to the garden to select; consequently, as in all transactions where money is concerned, the French soldiers made a most awful clamour, most of them, being more than half drunk, made it worse. One fellow made so much noise as to attract the attention of French councillors sitting in debate within the *auberge*, and an officer was sent to see what was the matter.

I shall never forget his face of astonishment when he looked in at the doorway, and saw such a large collection of French dragoons. On questioning me, I told him what they were; he either could not or would not believe it possible, and wished me to send them away. That I told him I dare not do; however, he returned to the house, shortly coming back accompanied by a staff-officer from our headquarters, who told me I had better indulge their wish and let the Frenchmen return to their regiments, on which the whole were paraded and asked by the officer, how they came there. All of them declared they had been made prisoners – of course they were allowed to decamp, which, I must say, I regretted, as I had quite made up my mind to have selected a good horse out of the lot.

The Treaty of Evacuation was completed that evening; the French troops commenced their march, and in the morning the light division advanced and took possession of the barrier Louis Quinze.

My party were ordered to the rear to join the regiment; but I took advantage of being so far in front, to get the first peep at Paris; and, accompanied by Colonel Reynell of the 71st – now Sir Thomas – got permission, under the rose, to pass the pickets of the 52nd.[40]

It may have been about 7 a.m. when we entered the front of the Tuilleries. I was quite a stranger to the place, never having been in Paris before, not so the colonel, who was well acquainted with the different streets and cafés, etc.

He proposed that we should have some breakfast at some particular house he named. On our way I could not help remarking, it looked like the city of the dead, not a soul to be seen, the windows of the houses and shops all closed – a melancholy appearance reigned throughout the whole line, so much so that I observed to my companion: 'This looks as if it is going to be a second Moscow affair.'

We stopped at a house near the Palais Royale where we procured a breakfast; but the same silence was there, and a sullen look in the face of the man who served us with what we had made the thing very unpleasant.

On mounting our horses, to return to the barrier, the scene was altered, we may have been absent about an hour, but that hour had worked wonders; the places we had passed so shortly before quite deserted, were now thronged with gaily dressed crowds hurrying on towards the hotel which was to have the honour of being occupied by the Duke of Wellington. He was on the point of making his entry, as we got to the Place Louis Quinze, amidst 'Vivas' and shouts from the multitude that had assembled to view the conqueror of their Emperor.

Towards afternoon the Allied Sovereigns also entered, viz., the Emperor Alexander of Russia and the King of Prussia. Paris was all alive!

The 12th were encamped for the night in what is called the Bois de Boulogne. The next day we retired and took up our quarters in the village of Neuilly; we took duty in rotation with the two other regiments of the brigade, making our turn every third day.

Our time was spent, as a matter of course, very pleasantly, being in such a neighbourhood. Everything to be seen was new and interesting, my quarters were in the house of a most amiable and kind old gentleman and his wife. About this time long and constant fatigue and sleeping out at night, while suffering from a cold, brought on a sharp attack of fever, which confined me to my bed for some days; but the great attention I received from the good people, in whose house I was

---

40   Thomas Reynell had commanded the 71st at Waterloo, having previously served in the Peninsula from January 1809-April 1811. He was wounded at Waterloo but on returning to duty superseded Colborne, his junior, as commander of the 3rd Brigade in Adam's continued absence. 'Under the rose' signifies *sub rosa*, or in secret.

quartered, and my naturally good constitution, shook off the fever, and I resumed my duties, or, rather, pleasures – as our duties were all ended. In the wood at one side of the road, were encamped a large party of the Cossacks of the Don, our regiment, when on duty, occupied the other.

At the fashionable time of the day for the Parisians to turn out, the walks were crowded with persons on horseback and on foot, to gaze at their invaders. Our amusement was to seat ourselves on the top of one of the many barriers on the sides of the road, and look at them passing us, as we termed it, in review order.

On one of these occasions a smart, dapper-looking fellow kept showing himself off on horse-back, and seemed to have such a good opinion of both himself and the animal he rode, that I could not resist the temptation of asking him if he particularly wished to become better acquainted, that he passed so often. To my surprise and that of my companions, instead of being offended at my remark, he answered: 'Yes, I should like to become better acquainted.'

The ice once broken we descended from the barrier and drew round our new friend. He was asked if his nag was a good one. He could do everything but speak, he declared, and was the best in France. I said: 'Well, prove the assertion by riding him over that gate'; pointing to the barrier where we had been seated, on which he immediately dismounted, and, in the most polite manner, offered to hold the stirrup for me to mount and perform the feat I had requested him to perform.

The laugh was now against me. However, he gave me a very pressing invitation to visit him at his own house and become better acquainted. That I agreed to do, and accepted his request to breakfast with him the next day, when our regiment went off duty.

On taking his leave and presenting his card, conceive my astonishment when I found the man I had been taking so much liberty with was a well-known prince, and no less a personage than a brother-in-law of the Duke of Cumberland.[41]

Next forenoon, as arranged, I found my way to his house, where a breakfast in first-rate style was ready and waiting. He received me most cordially and kindly, and after breakfast took me to see his numerous stud, which, to my surprise, I found to consist of about thirty horses taken from the 'Greys' when their riders were killed in the charge on the field of Waterloo.

I asked him if he were not afraid to show those horses to me, he answered: 'No, it is the chances of war which has put them in my stable.' He had bought them at very low prices from different soldiers who had brought them off as prizes.

41 Prince Ernest Augustus, Duke of Cumberland and Teviotdale, fifth son of George III, had married Frederica of Mecklenburg-Strelitz in May 1815. The new Duchess of Cumberland had one living brother and one half-brother. The latter was a general in the Prussian service and his command was not involved in the Hundred Days campaign, so it is to be inferred that Hay encountered the former: Georg, Hereditary Prince of Mecklenburg-Strelitz.

He told me he was to start for England that evening, and, in the most gracious manner, desired me to make his house my home during his absence; but this condescension and civility I did not of course accept, although I bought from him a very handsome thorough-bred mare which, two days after, nearly made me pay for my bargain with my life.

There was a large meadow on the left bank of the Seine, near our cantonment, where the regiment used to assemble for parade; two days after the purchase of the mare I mounted her for this parade.

On going to inspect the troop, the sergeant presented me with the slate, to look at which I laid my reins on the mare's neck; before I could recover them she started at the top of her speed to the astonishment of all present, on she went right across the great meadow; I conceived it must have been my sword that caused the sudden fright, so I undid it and let it drop. But no; away she went on her headlong career. I had quite made up my mind we were in for a drowning match, the bank at the place she was making for may have been at least forty feet above the water's edge, and I saw no chance of escape, when, within five yards of the brink, the animal stopped short as if she had been shot. I was off her back in a moment; there she stood trembling, I turned her head round, mounted, and rode quietly back, to be congratulated on my narrow escape. I afterwards found it was caused by the rattle of the paper I had in my hand, as a similar thing occurred at another time when a soldier handed me a letter; in all other respects I found her most docile.

To relate even a moiety of our pastimes in the shape of duties or pleasures during our sojourn so near the French capital would tend to no information, I, therefore, content myself by merely stating we enjoyed ourselves to our heart's content, seeing sights, etc.

One or two good reviews of all the troops quartered in the neighbourhood took place, on which occasions the remarks of surprise, expressed by the French soldiers and spectators, were both gratifying and curious to hear, expressing wonder to each other, as the different regiments of infantry passed by, how it could possibly be that such small men could have beaten the French Imperial Guards at Waterloo!

I will relate one incident that happened before leaving Paris, showing the French character in those days and the effect of a little wholesome chastisement on their braggadocio manner.

With a brother officer, now no more – Lieutenant Calderwood – I proceeded to Paris one evening to dine and go to the opera.[42] On leaving the café we hired a coach to convey us there, and made an agreement with the driver that he was to return for us at a stated hour, and take us back to our quarters at Neuilly – about four miles – on being paid a sum stipulated for.

---

42   Lieutenant James Calderwood had served in the Peninsula with the 12th Light Dragoons from May 1812 until the end of the war. He did not serve at Waterloo, re-joining the active portion of the regiment after the battle.

The man was true to his engagement so far, as, on coming out of the theatre, we found the coach in readiness. It turned out a very wet night, and we congratulated ourselves on taking our seats, at having sent our horses home, and being able to return to our quarters under cover.

The man who drove us was dressed in the fashion of the day with French coachmen of the better class, with a large three-cornered cocked hat and big wig. On we went as far as the Pont de Neuilly, about two miles from Paris. At the gate was a guard of Prussian soldiers, here we came to a dead stop, and the man, getting off his box, opened the carriage door, and said, in a very polite French way, he requested we would descend as the night was so very wet he could not think of proceeding further!

Our astonishment was great at his coolness, and, of course, we remonstrated; he said he would not go on. He did not ask for payment as he had broken his contract, but that his horses were tired and he was wet and wished to return to Paris. We endeavoured to reason with the fellow but all to no purpose.

Hearing the altercation, the Prussian guard had assembled and stood smoking their pipes and looking on, of course not understanding the nature of the dispute. After the loss of at least a quarter of an hour in idle persuasion, I got out of the carriage determined to get on the box and drive on myself; but, before ascending to the seat, I repeated my request that he would go on and fulfil his bargain, 'No, monsieur!' was the only reply, on which I gave him a straightforward hit under the ear, that sent him several yards sprawling in the road right among the Prussian soldiers; from thence he got several kicks, with the words, *donner und blitzen, allez.*[43]

I certainly expected nothing less than to have been charged with the assault and given into the custody of the officer of the guard; therefore, conceive my astonishment at the fellow coolly picking himself up, wiping the blood from his face with one hand, holding his hat in the other, begging pardon, and requesting I would get in and be seated, which I did, at the same time showing a half-drawn sword, telling him if he attempted to turn after I got in, or did not proceed direct to our destination, the consequence would be that the sword would be sheathed in his fat body.

The door was shut, he got on his box, and drove to the further side of the bridge about two miles distant, pulled up, and enquired for further orders, that I told him was unnecessary, as our contract was finished. So frightened was the rascally Frenchman, that he offered to return the money paid for the journey. It was clearly a proof to me that there was only one way to treat a Frenchman; and I adopted afterwards the words *il faut* for any request I had to make.[44]

The forage for the horses was required in such large quantities, and the summer drawing to a close, that, in order to obtain it, it was decided, about the end of

---

43 That is to say, 'thunder and lightning' (German), 'go' (French).
44 The use of '*Il Faut*' in this sense signifies 'you must'.

August, the British cavalry should leave the neighbourhood of the capital and take up cantonments in different parts of the country, some distance from Paris. The destination of our brigade was Normandy.

Our march proceeded by easy stages through the different districts of France without any particular incidents worthy of note. We reached the small town of Forges d'Eau, in which the headquarters of the 12th, with two troops, were to be cantoned, the remaining troops of the regiment occupying the surrounding villages. I was posted with the left squadron at a place called Cailly-Fontaine.[45]

There I was quartered at the house of an old widow lady, whose only son had been killed at Waterloo. Poor woman! she did all in her power to make us at home and comfortable under her hospitable roof. She lent me an old double-barrelled gun, that had been the property of her son, and assisted me in getting a dog, so, by equipping myself in a sort of French *jacquet de chasse*, I was delighted to find myself, once more, free from the restraints of military life in a large garrison town and able to enjoy, what I considered at the time, the greatest happiness – field sports – unrestrained by game laws.

As we were in what is termed, 'winter quarters after a campaign,' our duties as soldiers were very light; our amusements consisted of shooting quails, which were most abundant in the neighbourhood, and going about visiting our brother officers quartered in other parts of the district.

From their former hard work amongst the French, as enemies, our men could never reconcile themselves to the idea of being friends now; consequently, to hit or shoot a Frenchman was of little moment.

One man, named Power, in my troop – who has been mentioned in a former part of this for his gallant conduct at Waterloo when under my observation – was one of those who took to the road. He waylaid two men one night and took from them some money, but the men gallantly defending themselves wounded Power, which was the cause of his being arrested. He was brought to meet a general court-martial and sentenced to receive a thousand lashes; which punishment, as I have before told, he received without uttering a sound.[46]

On another occasion a party of us had ridden over to the headquarters canton-ment to enjoy a French horse-fair and dine with our brother officers living there.

---

45   Fontaine-le-Bourg, eleven miles north of Rouen. Forges-les-Eaux, site of the regimental headquarters, is situated 18 miles to the east.

46   Power was tried for 'Robbery &c.' at Abbeville on 2 October 1815 and sentenced to 1,000 lashes. Interestingly, his co-accused, Private Forrest, is noted in the official register as 'acquitted and admitted evidence'. This could indicate that he was Power's accomplice and saved himself by testifying against him, or, alternatively, that he was an innocent bystander and that the circumstances of his alibi in some way incriminated Power, perhaps because he was a witness to the incident. See TNA, WO90/1, Judge Advocate General's Office: General Courts Martial Registers, Abroad, 1796-1825. I am obliged to Eamonn O'Keeffe for his advice and assistance in trying to establish the possible facts from this sparse record.

On returning at night, I saw something lying in the road, and dismounted to see what it was. I found a new hat! and said to one of my companions, in a joke: 'I will take this home.' But we had not proceeded very far when, to our horror, we found the poor owner of the hat, a lifeless corpse, in the middle of the road, having been shot through the head by one of our dragoons a few minutes before. The man, hearing the approach of our horses, had taken to flight before being able to effect the rifling of his victim.

We returned immediately to report the circumstance and to take steps to secure the men implicated in the murder. Two men were confined on strong suspicion of being the aggressors; indeed no one doubted their guilt but, for want of sufficient evidence, after six months' confinement both were released.

Our next change of quarters, sometime during the month of November, was to Picardy. Our headquarters being at a small town called Fruges; about twelve miles from thence I was quartered at a village called Brugesville, some twenty miles from Rouen.[47]

There the regiment agreed to establish a pack of foxhounds, and, after some trouble and considerable expense, procured about twenty couple, with a huntsman – old John Major – from England. I had the honour of having them put under my particular care during the time I was at Brugesville. About this time I had the misfortune to be ordered on one of those unpleasant duties – a general court-martial – and was called on to proceed to Amiens, the headquarters of the 23rd Light Dragoons. On my return, after an absence of three weeks, I found my regiment had again changed their cantonments and had headquarters at Neufchatel en Brai, and, on my arrival, instead of finding myself quietly located in a small un-sophisticated cottage, I was informed, to my horror, that my quarters, with a detachment of thirty men, with the hounds, were at the Chateau of Monsieur Davie – a large and rich landed proprietor.[48]

The snow was deep on the ground, and the days at their shortest; therefore, finding myself domiciled in the midst of a French family of distinction, and not being able to converse with them fluently in French, was a sad drawback to my comfort. Although I received great kindness and attention from the whole family, I quite made up my mind to torment my good-natured old commanding officer, Colonel Bridger, till he gave his consent to my finding some other more congenial quarters. As he never could refuse to do a kind action, his permission was soon obtained.

No doubt to the great relief of Monsieur Davie as well as myself, after a sojourn of some two or three weeks with him, I one day discovered, about twenty miles

47 Fruges is situated some 25 miles south-east of Boulogne; 'Brugesville' cannot be located, but it is physically impossible for any location to be both 12 miles from Fruges and 20 miles from Rouen as those two places are separated by nearly 100 miles.
48 Neufchâtel-en-Bray, 25 miles north-east of Rouen.

distant from his house, while hunting, a large, very old, uninhabited mansion; which, on inspection, I found to be the very place for my purpose. The village, or, rather, hamlet, was named St. Cyre, after the marquis of that name; the old padre had the sole charge of the chateau and the estate – as good a creature as ever lived.[49] To him I immediately made my application, he went about with me himself to look over the accommodation which, in my opinion, was super-excellent, about fifty rooms in a very large building, all well-furnished, but had not been occupied since the revolution of 1792, when the family emigrated to England, and the property was only restored to them in 1814, on the return of the Royal family to France.

Having installed myself and men in our new quarters, and the weather having become open and mild, hunting was the order of the day.

There being lots of beds in the house for any of our brother officers from other quarters, and most capital wine in the marquis's cellars; we had no lack of society, and time passed very delightfully, but, like most other pleasures, it had its end, and one morning I got the order to march my detachment and join headquarters in Neufchatel.

Thus ended the year 1815.

In the spring of 1816, the 12th were removed to join another brigade, under the command of Sir H. Vivian – late Lord Vivian.[50] The hounds were handed over to the officers of the 52nd, and we were directed to concentrate for drills.

Our change of quarters was to the Paz de Calais; the headquarters of the 12th were at a small town, named Davres, about twelve miles from Boulogne.[51]

My troop was at a wretched village some eight miles from Davres, and I took up my abode at a farmhouse, with a detachment of men, to enable me to enjoy the country and at the same time be at a distance from my captain, who, although a good fellow, was too fond of long sittings after dinner to suit my health; it was therefore only occasionally he could press me into the service to dine with him.

When he did so, being at a distance was a good excuse to get off early, to reach home before dark, as the whole country was infested with the disbanded soldiers of the Imperial Army, who were ready to take a shot at British officers whenever opportunity offered. Besides, the lanes, which were narrow and very dark, from the foliage, were overrun by wolves, which had followed the army.

One night, however, having been persuaded to remain late, I was proceeding home on a very lazy piebald pony I had as a hack, when I came to a long, dark, avenue leading up to the house; nearly half-asleep, I was aroused by the sudden

---

49 This would seem to be the village of Saint-Saire, four miles south-east of Neufchâtel-en-Bray.
50 Sir Richard Hussey Vivian had, as noted, previously commanded the 6th Cavalry Brigade during the Waterloo campaign. His new command in the reduced Army of Occupation was denominated the 2nd Cavalry Brigade and was composed of the 7th and 18th Hussars as well as the 12th Light Dragoons.
51 The location in fact Desvres, located as Hay says.

stoppage of my horse and his snorting and wanting to turn back – a most unusual event with him, as in general he began to hurry – when so near home. After considerable urging with whip and spur, off he started, to my astonishment, at runaway pace, till he reached the stable door, I remarked to the groom: 'What can have come over the pony to-night, he has actually run away with me.'

The animal was as wet as if he had been in a river, and trembling all over; I thought no more of it and went to bed. In about two hours I was disturbed by one of the young men of the farm coming into my room to invite me to accompany them in a *chasse au loup*. A she wolf with two cubs had been in the farmyard, and killed a sheep and some lambs. This, then, accounted for the proceedings of my poor horse, as the brute must have been in the lane when I passed through towards the house.

Towards autumn of this year, all the allied, cavalry and artillery were ordered to assemble for a grand review on the plain near Valenciennes. Thence we marched, and remained for about a month. It was truly a grand sight. About fifty thousand cavalry, of all the nations composing the army of occupation, on the same field. I had a good opportunity of seeing the spectacle to advantage, having been the officer selected to attend the general commanding the cavalry – Lord Combermere.[52]

After the reviews were over we returned to our old quarters, my troop going to Davres, and the headquarters to villages on the outskirts of Boulogne. My mother and sisters had been for some time wishing me to apply for leave, to enable me to visit home once more. Although at all times, disinclined to leave my regiment, it was a duty I owed both to them and myself; I, therefore, made an application about the end of July and obtained leave of absence for three months; but, before I had enjoyed the pleasures of home for three weeks, I received the appointment of *aide-de-camp* on the staff of the Earl of Dalhousie, then Lieutenant-Governor of Nova Scotia.

---

52   Lt. General Lord Combermere – the title was bestowed upon Stapleton Cotton in 1814, so Hay is now correct to use it – had taken over the command of Wellington's cavalry after Uxbridge was wounded at Waterloo, and retained this post in the Army of Occupation. The review to which Hay refers took place in October 1816. See Thomas Dwight Veve, *The Duke of Wellington and the British Army of Occupation in France, 1815-1818* (Westport: Greenwood, 1992). pp.37-39, 46

4

Nova Scotia and Canada 1817-1823[1]

On August 10, 1817, I once again left Spott and all most dear to me, to take up my appointment as *aide-de-camp* on the staff of the Earl of Dalhousie, obtaining a passage in the government frigate *Forth*, commanded by Sir J. Louis.[2]

After a long but most agreeable voyage, having remained a week at the island of Madeira, we arrived within sight of the rock-bound and barren coast of Nova Scotia, on a beautiful day towards the end of October, going with every sail set. Towards 10 p.m. the ship was run on the Thrumcap Shoal, some twenty miles from her destination, and there we remained all night, the wind getting up and the weather looking threatening, made our position and chance of ever getting off a bad one; however, after she had been lightened of her guns and masts, she was hoved off, and towed up to Halifax – a wreck.[3]

Lord and Lady Dalhousie had gone to their country house near Windsor; therefore, for some weeks, I had the Government House to myself.[4]

A Nova Scotian life, after my recent experience of the more active one of a soldier on service, furnishes but few interesting incidents; therefore; suffice it to be said, I had the honour and happiness to be on the staff of one of the very best,

---

1   The material in this chapter was originally presented under this title as Part II of the work, the preceding chapters all being lumped together as Part I, with a note by Hay's daughter saying: 'Circumstances proved this to be the conclusion of my father's experiences on "Active Service"; but the following notes of his subsequent career in Nova Scotia and Canada may be of interest'. Strictly speaking, the title ought to be 'Nova Scotia and the Canadas' since, at the time of Hay's service in British North America, Upper and Lower Canada were separate provinces. The former comprised the southern part of what is now Ontario, the latter present-day Quebec. I must again express my thanks to Canadian scholar Eamonn O'Keeffe for his assistance in compiling the notes to this chapter.
2   HMS *Forth* was a 50-gun heavy frigate, one of several built to counter the similar ships fielded by the United States Navy in the War of 1812. Her commanding officer was Captain Sir John Louis.
3   The Thrumcap Shoal lies off the entrance to Halifax harbour. The damage was evidently severe, as the *Forth* was sold out of service in 1819 after a career of only six years.
4   Christian Ramsay (née Broun), Countess of Dalhousie, came from an old Scots legal family and was a keen naturalist who accompanied her husband in the series of overseas postings (Nova Scotia, Canada, and India) that made up his post-1815 career.

most high-minded, and truly noble General officers that ever lived; his only fault was over-generosity – if, indeed, that can be counted one. He was too apt to judge others by himself – having neither guile nor dissimulation in his character, he forgot that many others were not of the same composition.

With him and Lady Dalhousie I had not only the honour of acting, from the day I joined his staff, as an *aide-de-camp*, but as the constant companion to both; therefore, no one could have had better opportunities afforded him, of clearly estimating these two most noble and amiable people.

Towards the autumn of 1817, Sir John Sherbrook, Governor-General of Canada, returned to England, and no one ever doubted but that the Earl of Dalhousie would follow to Quebec as his successor; therefore, it may be well believed the disappointment and indignation it caused when intelligence arrived that His Grace the Duke of Richmond had received the appointment.[5]

My noble-minded senior could not brook such an uncalled for insult, and prepared to tender his resignation. But by this time winter had set in and navigation was closed; he, therefore, proposed to take advantage of being on that side of the Atlantic Ocean, to visit Canada and the Falls of Niagara before his return to England; consequently, postponed his resolution to throw up his command till he had done so.

The winter of 1817 passed in the most agreeable and delightful way, all being so new to me, sleighing and driving during the day, dinner-parties and balls in the evening.

In the spring of 1818, I accompanied Lord and Lady Dalhousie to Bermuda, where we went on a visit to Admiral Sir David Milne, remaining there about three weeks. During our voyage we encountered one of the most awful storms I ever witnessed or could have imagined.[6]

About the month of May the party, consisting of Lord and Lady Dalhousie, their two children, Colonel Cooper, Lord Schomberg Kerr, and myself, embarked on board the *Athol* frigate, commanded by Captain E. Collier, and sailed for Quebec, accompanied by the *Cabustre*, a small schooner attached to the lieutenant-governor's suite for his use in visiting different parts of the coast under his command.[7]

5   General Sir John Coape Sherbrooke had served as Lieutenant Governor of Nova Scotia 1811-16 and as Governor General of British North America 1816-18, although his name may be more familiar through his role as second in command of the British forces in early stages of the Peninsular War. General Charles Lennox, 4th Duke of Richmond had enjoyed a long military career but seen little active service, having spent the years 1807-1813 as Lord Lieutenant of Ireland. His family travelled to the continent in 1815 largely for financial reasons, where his wife hosted the famous ball of 15 June and he himself observed the fighting at Waterloo as a spectator.
6   Rear Admiral Sir David Milne had been a noted frigate-captain in the earlier stages of the wars against France. After obtaining flag rank in 1814 he served in the Algiers expedition of 1816 before being appointed to command the North American Station later that year.
7   HMS *Athol* was a sixth-rate frigate, or corvette, rated at 28 guns and launched in 1816. Hay's fellow-aides, named here, were Sir George Couper – not Cooper – who has already made an appearance in

On our arrival at Quebec it was ascertained the Duke of Richmond had commenced his journey, to make an inspection of some new townships at the time about to be laid out and, having left the castle (the residence of the governor-general) ready for the reception of Lord Dalhousie, intended to await his arrival at Kingston, in Upper Canada.[8]

After a sojourn of two or three days at Quebec, we embarked on board one of the River St. Lawrence steamboats, on our way to Montreal.[9] There we also remained two days.

Thence we proceeded in open bateaux, or flat boats, from St. Ann's to Kingston, where we overtook the Duke of Richmond, who was staying with Sir F. Maitland, then lieutenant-governor of that province;[10] and with his grace we embarked again in one of the lake steamboats, which was to convey him to Toronto.[11] Our party, consisting of the staff of both generals, was a large one. The time was spent most agreeably during the short voyage of two days – shooting at marks with rifles and such like amusements.

I observed the duke wore his arm in a sling, and looked thoughtful – more so than I should have expected of him, knowing his character.

During the shooting he made me shoot for him, from his inability to use his hand, and, extraordinary to say, I suppose, from the excellence of his rifle, I won every pool, beating the other competitors at the first shot; and always, when drawing lots who should commence, gaining the longest lot, which prevented others ever getting a chance, till it was agreed I should take the last – still I beat them all.

At the town of York, the duke and his staff went on shore, and we proceeded to Fort St. George [sic – Fort George] at the mouth of the Niagara river, where we remained one day; from thence we went to the Falls of Niagara; and took up our quarters at an inn, kept by a man named Forsyth, where we remained about a week.[12]

---

this narrative and Lieutenant Lord Schomberg Robert Kerr, second son of the 6th Marquess of Lothian. Hay places his account of this trip in 1818, but in fact he is a year adrift in his chronology and the events that follow took place in 1819.

8   The castle referred to was the Château Saint-Louis, originally the residence of the Governor General of New France and subsequently of British Governors.

9   These steamboats were a very new invention, the first having appeared on Canadian inland waters during the previous decade.

10 The Lieutenant Governor of Upper Canada was Sir Peregrine – the 'F' is evidently a typographical error – Maitland, of Waterloo fame, who was also Richmond's son-in-law having married the Duke's daughter Lady Sarah Lennox in 1815.

11 Hay is here using a name that was not then in use. Toronto was not so named until 1834 and was previously known as York, which name Hay himself uses later in his account.

12 William Forsyth (1771-1841), an American-born entrepreneur with a shady background that may or may not have included espionage during the War of 1812 and smuggling thereafter, did much to popularise the Niagara Falls as a tourist destination.

Lord Dalhousie and his party returned by the route we came; while Lord S. Kerr, two others, and myself, with a servant, were to take our way, making a tour through the States, to New York, and thence to embark for Halifax.

Our stay at Forsyth's hotel and a delay of two days at the town of Buffalo, gave us a sample of what we had often heard and read about, *i.e.*, Yankee inquisitiveness; we were soon discovered to be strangers, and every fellow thought it fine to ask questions as to what we were, what we wanted, where we were going, etc.

The pest was so great that we determined, for the sake of a little amusement, to deceive our inquisitors as much as we could, and assume characters. The part that fell to my rôle was that of a trader, returning from a trading expedition amongst the Indians; accordingly, we took our places in the common stage-coach of the country, a long cumbrous vehicle carrying, on swinging benches, about sixteen passengers, over the very worst of roads. We adapted our conversation as much as we could to surprise and excite our fellow travellers, one man kept on constantly urging all sorts of questions, but could never get a satisfactory reply.

One Sunday morning we stopped to breakfast and change horses, this enquirer went up to my servant, who happened to be a very fat man, and, I noticed, he was pressing him very hard on some subject; I went up to hear what he was urging, and found he was inviting him to come into the room to breakfast, and, turning to me, said: 'I cannot understand this man, since we started on the journey three days since he has never sat down, that I could observe, to a single meal, but always keeps to himself', I could not resist the opportunity of getting a rise out of the Yankee, so, beckoning him to one side, I informed him, putting on a very serious manner: 'You had much better not annoy that person with questions, perhaps you have not found out who he is'. 'No; that is what I want', was his reply. 'Well, he is a Roman Catholic priest, and he is a hermit, we are all Catholics and he our confessor, and he has no communication, nor will he eat at the same table, with you heretics. He permits us, when on a journey, to do so, and gives us absolution afterwards'.

The man looked at me for a moment in silence with astonishment in his countenance, and exclaimed: '*Who* you are, and *what* you are, I cannot make out! I started in the same coach with you intending to have branched off at such-and-such a place, to go to Boston, and I have come some two hundred miles out of my way; but the longer I am with you the further I seem to get from knowing more about you. I guess I am as much at a loss as when we set out; I, therefore, reckon I'll go no further!'

The Yankee kept his word, and was very sulky all breakfast-time, and had actually to wait the arrival of some conveyance to enable him to retrace the steps he had been led out of his way by curiosity.

We stayed a couple of days at Albery [sic – Albany], thence went to the springs of Balstone [sic – Ballston] and Saratoga, the battle ground and defeat of the British arms during the American rebellion. The weather was dreadfully hot and the place full of company, of which I soon tired; and therefore left my companions, after a day or two's sojourn, and took my way to New York.

One adventure I met with there, from the same Yankee curiosity, which it is but fair to tell as it speaks to the credit of the parties and shows their curiosity may often be meant with kind intention, although misunderstood by strangers. I had been recommended to put up at the boarding-house of a Mrs. Wilkinson, to which I proceeded on my arrival. I was introduced into the sitting-room, till such time as a bedroom was ready for me to go and dress; I observed while there two men in conversation, of whom I took no notice; my servant having reported my things in readiness, I left the room.

After making myself tidy, I strolled out to look about the town; when, coming down one of the streets, I was met by a tall, elderly, well-dressed man, who, after looking hard at me, exclaimed: 'I guess I saw you in Mrs. Wilkinson's boarding-house?' My answer was: 'Very likely you did, as I have taken a room there'. 'I suppose you are a stranger in New York?' I replied: 'Yes, I am'. Then he said: 'Would you like to go to the commercial-rooms?' 'Very much', said I. So away we went. He introduced me, asking my name, as his friend; and told me he reckoned it was cooler and pleasanter there than walking the streets in the sun, to which I assented. I then saw no more of my acquaintance, he having disappeared among the numbers assembled to read and lounge about. While sitting after dinner, a servant came to tell me a lady had called to see me. I was astonished, for I knew not a living soul in the place. However, I attended the call of the fair one, who introduced herself by saying her father was the person I had met in the morning who introduced me to the commercial-rooms, that he regretted an engagement prevented his calling on me himself.

He had sent her with a letter, addressed to a friend of his at Boardington, introducing me as his particular acquaintance, in whom he was interested, and requested his friend to show me every civility for his sake; particularly, to introduce me to Joseph Bonaparte, who lived in the neighbourhood, and the individual to whom this was addressed was the medical man who attended the family of the ex-king.[13]

I felt greatly gratified by this attention from a perfect stranger, and he an American; but conceive my further astonishment when this was followed up by my having a most polite letter sent me by the commodore in command at the dockyard, by a lieutenant in the Navy, inviting me to breakfast on board the steam frigate – at that time one of the wonders of the day – and inspect all that was worth seeing of their shipping.[14]

---

13   Joseph Bonaparte, erstwhile King of Spain and Naples, lived in exile in the United States 1817-1832, for part of the time at Bordentown, New Jersey (Hay's 'Boardington').

14   The 'steam frigate' was in fact a steam-propelled floating battery constructed for the defence of New York harbour but finished too late to see action in the War of 1812. Designed by Robert Fulton, and renamed after him following his death having originally gone by the name *Demologos*, the ship was a catamaran with a paddle-wheel placed between the two hulls where it was protected from enemy fire and did not interfere with the designed armament of 30 cannon.

For this purpose he begged to be allowed to place his own boat at my disposal; in fact, my newly made friend – Dr. Macleod – took every trouble to show me the most marked attention and kindness, which most justly impressed me with the kind feeling of the Americans, who can be and are so hospitable to strangers, and convinced me that what appears to us obtrusive curiosity, is often very differently meant by them, which was certainly proved in my case.

After a stay of about eleven days in New York, I proceeded to visit Philadelphia; and from thence returned and took my passage in the packet *en route* to Halifax, N.S., at which place I was most kindly welcomed by my General and Lady Dalhousie. The autumn had now set in, and the weather, as is the case in that country, was particularly fine.

His lordship, having finished his despatches, amongst which was the resignation of his appointment, and got everything in readiness for the packet, which was to sail for England in October, proposed to help pass the time by making a shooting and fishing excursion into the interior of the provinces for a few weeks, giving me directions to select a few friends as companions, and to make the necessary preparations for the purpose.

Accompanied by Admiral Milne and several others, we spent a very pleasant three weeks in visiting different localities, remaining for a day or two at a time at the best country inns to be found, where shooting and fishing could be had in the neighbourhood.

On our way back to Halifax we stopped to pay a visit to the country seat of the attorney-general, his lordship's intention being to remain there two days, and get to Halifax in time to send off his letters, etc., by the packet.

Mr. Uniack was himself one of the most clever, amusing, and interesting persons that could be possibly imagined in any society, full of anecdotes, and knowing right well how to tell them.[15]

He had assembled all his guests round a log fire in his smoking-room, each with his pipe or cigar and a goodly supply of whisky and rum on the round table, and we were fully prepared for an evening's entertainment. (The house I, must observe stands in a very lone situation, miles from any other, surrounded by two-thirds forest and lake, and is twenty-two miles from Halifax.)

Suddenly a tremendous knocking at the front door startled us and made each one look at his neighbour with a sort of dread that something unexpected and unpleasant had occurred, to cause so unwelcome a disturbance at twelve o'clock at night.

When the door was opened, an officer in uniform entered, and enquired for the Earl of Dalhousie. Being told he was within, he said he had brought despatches of importance from Quebec. On this his lordship expressed his hope that he had left

---

15 Richard John Uniacke had served as Attorney General of Nova Scotia since 1797. His estate at Mount Uniacke, twenty-five miles south of Halifax, is now preserved as a museum.

the Duke of Richmond well. Conceive our astonishment, when the answer to this was: 'The Duke is no more!'

It appeared on explanation that his grace had been suffering much when he parted with us, as before mentioned, at Kingston, Upper Canada.

Prior to leaving Sorel (or William Henry as it is commonly called), which was the country seat of the governor, he had his hand bitten by a tame fox he kept as a pet, this fully accounted for the lowness of spirits, I had already observed, and his not being able to use his rifle, when he got me to shoot for him on board the steamer.

As it may be interesting, I will give a short account of his melancholy end I had from an eyewitness of the sad event.

On leaving our party, he proceeded with the quarter-master-general and his military escort on a tour through some new settlements. Towards the end of his first day's journey, he complained – an unusual circumstance with him – of great fatigue and of feeling unwell, and seemed in very low spirits; however, on arriving at the resting-place for the night, he invited a number of half-pay officers and others settled there, to dine with him.

It appears that at dinner he first showed signs of what was really the matter with him; although none present had the slightest idea of the horrible truth, as at table, when wine was poured into his glass, he could not convey it to his lips and struggled hard to conceal what he himself must have been aware of and most dreaded.

He retired early to lie down, but, I believe, never slept; by daybreak he expressed a wish to proceed on his journey, and on foot, refusing the use of a horse which some of his officers had provided for him. He had not got far from the log house, where the party had rested for the night, when he put his foot on the stump of an old tree, he slipped, and caused some water underneath to splash up, causing the first paroxysm to show itself, on which he fainted, and was conveyed by his followers to the brink of the lake where there was a small canoe, in which he was placed with the intention of conveying him to the nearest place – some twenty miles off – where assistance could be obtained; but the water again had such an effect on his nerves that he was landed.

On regaining the ground, he bounded off like a boy, and cleared in his course a rail, or gate, of considerable height, on the other side of which he fell exhausted, and, on his staff coming up they found him in a state of raving madness.

In a few minutes, however, he recovered himself and became quite sensible, took leave of those about him, and sent messages to his family, who were awaiting his return to receive him with honours, at Montreal.

For the first time he mentioned the bite of the fox, and what he well knew to be the consequences, and from which he was now preparing to meet his death; in a few minutes another fit came on, and he died.[16]

---

16 Hay's account corresponds to the general narrative of the events leading up to the Duke's death on 28 August 1819 and agrees with the consensus that it was the rabid bite of his pet fox that brought about his demise, rather than that of a dog as is suggested by some accounts.

This caused, as you can well believe, great sorrow to all our party assembled; and, with thoughts now very differently directed, we betook ourselves to our rooms, Lord Dalhousie and myself to start for Halifax at daybreak.

We arrived there to breakfast, and brought with us the first intelligence of the governor-general's death. The packet was stopped to give his lordship time to alter his despatches, and send home the accounts to the Government.

Shortly after the sailing of the packet, which brought it nearly to November, winter began, and our pastime, as in the former year, went on, though of course awaiting with considerable anxiety news from England, regarding the decision of the home Government as to who was to succeed the late Duke of Richmond in Canada.

Thus ended 1818.

In January, 1819 [sic – 1820: Hay's chronology is still a year adrift], Lord Dalhousie received his appointment as Governor-general and Commander-in-chief. Colonel Cooper, first *aide-de-camp* – now Sir George – left his lordship's staff about this time, and I succeeded to the charges vested in him.

Towards the end of May, the governor, his family, and staff embarked on board the *Newcastle*, a fifty-gun frigate, and sailed for Quebec.[17] After a short and pleasant passage we again came to anchor in the River St. Lawrence.

Lord Dalhousie was sworn in next day, and we took up our quarters in the Chateau de St. Louis. After a sojourn of about six weeks at Quebec, the weather becoming tremendously hot, Lord Dalhousie removed to the country quarters of the commander-in-chief, a small place called Sorel, where we spent the remainder of the summer, as I thought, stupidly enough.

The winters in Canada commence early, and, shortly after our return in the beginning of October, it set in with all its severity. Then, careering over snow roads on sleighs, tandem clubs, dinner-parties, and balls constituted the pastimes of the long winter in Quebec. The society was very good, and the residents most hospitable.

So ended 1819.

The races at Quebec, which were arranged to take place in June, 1820, over a very fair course, formed on the plain of Abraham, excited great interest; particularly as this season, for the first time, the governor gave a valuable silver cup to be run for.

Besides the horses belonging to the officers of the garrison and the inhabitants of the province, many others from the United States were expected to contend in the race for the prize.

---

17 HMS *Newcastle* was another of the heavy frigates built like the *Forth* in response to their American equivalents. Larger than the *Forth*, she had by this date been re-rated at 60 guns and served until 1850.

At that time, Lady Dalhousie had a little horse about fifteen hands of very ordinary appearance, which did not escape my observation from his particularly good shape and galloping qualities. He was not a pleasant horse for a lady, being unsafe to ride, from going in his walk too near the ground; I, therefore, proposed to his lordship that he should give me the horse and I would find one – better suited to her ladyship – in its place. Consequently, "Stag" was handed over to my stable. I soon gave him a gallop, and found I had been correct in my surmise as to his speed, and entered him for the cup; but all who saw the horse thought I was mad, as he could have no chance of winning amongst the highbred and fine-looking horses entered for that race.

The day of the trial duty arrived, when twelve horses started for the race, and twenty to one was bet against mine. But, to the astonishment of all parties and, I believe, of myself the most, Master Stag actually won in a canter, distancing all but two or three horses of the number that started against him. The cup, as you know, we still possess, which speaks for itself. That little horse was equally good and fast in harness; and he has often taken me across the snow, in a light sledge, twenty miles in the hour.

Soon after the Quebec races we took our departure for the country quarters at Sorel. From thence, about August, we visited the Falls of Niagara, and went through the different townships, then about to be settled for the first time.

Lady Dalhousie proceeded directly back to Sorel, while myself, with two or three others on his lordship's staff, crossed the country towards the Ottawa river, to pay a visit to one of the most extraordinary characters I ever, either before or since, met with, in the shape of an enterprising man – Philemon Wright – an American by birth. He had acted the part of under-secretary or clerk to General Washington during the Revolutionary war.

It may be interesting to give a short outline of this man's history, as he told it himself.

It appears that shortly after America had succeeded in disconnecting itself from this country, a continuance of his services not being required, he married, and bethought of settling himself and his family in some distant part of the country, where he could have the best chance of turning his active habits to account. Therefore, leaving his wife, who was not in a condition to travel, at Boston – his native place – he, accompanied by one follower, penetrated through the forests, surveying every part of the country for a locality on which he thought it would suit his purpose to form his future resting-place.[18]

18   Philemon Wright (1760-1839) enjoyed a varied life much as Hay outlines, founding the settlement of Wrightstown and running it, insofar as possible, as a personal fiefdom but in doing so driving the development of the Canadian lumber industry.

At last he reached the place of which I speak, which he called Phillipstown.[19] It was situated on the Falls of Chandier [sic – Chaudière] on the Ottawa river; at this spot the river is intersected with numerous shoots, from the rocky and uneven state of the bed at the bottom of a considerable rapid, going through and over these rocks and precipitating itself in a fall of some eighty or ninety feet.

The country in the neighbourhood, at the time, consisted of some natural plains of rich soil, surrounded by forest trees of hard wood – this was exactly the place suited to Wright's views.

With the river below and the lakes above, forming a first-rate highway, enabling him to carry out his plans of floating his timber to a marketable port; and the facility with which his quick eye perceived the natural shoots amongst the rocks, might be turned to fine account in forming, with little expense, natural conductors of water for the purpose of mill machinery.

Here, hundreds of miles from a living soul, he and his followers built themselves a hut, formed of the branches of trees, having at that time only their bill-hooks, which they had brought with them from Boston, to clear their way through the woods; however, with these he contrived to erect a place for living in, subsisting on fish caught in the lake above, and, having with considerable difficulty cleared, by cutting and burning, about two acres of ground and brushwood, they returned to the neighbourhood of Boston, where he provided himself with proper tools, seed potatoes, seed corn, and different articles wanted in a backwoodman's life.

He started again, towards the spring, to carry on fresh and vigorous operations; and that year he built a better description of log hut, farmed some cleared ground round it, cleared a lot more ground by burning the trees, and again returned to Boston in the autumn, having reaped the corn produced from the seed sown in the spring.

The potatoes reared, and placed in deep pits out of harm's way during the winter; he now considered he had a sufficient store and home for the reception of his family on his newly attained property.

In the spring of the next season he started, accompanied by his wife and child and two or three followers.

When we visited him in 1820, we found him in an excellent brick house, neatly laid out garden, and farm – containing three thousand acres of cleared land – some thousand head of cattle, horses, and pigs, the breeds all imported from England by himself.

The grounds about the falls, above and below, were covered with stores and houses for labourers, mills of different kinds, with the best machinery for cutting timber, grinding corn, etc,, etc.

---

19 Hay seems to have misremembered the name of Wright's eponymous settlement, which drew on his surname rather than his Christian name, but is correct in its location which is today part of Hull, Quebec.

He had five sons, each of whom was settled in a good house with a well-stocked farm – he had called his sons after the Roman Emperors, the eldest was Augustus Caesar, and so on.

His mode of procedure was an arbitrary one. At that time people, like himself, were in the habit of wandering into the interior in search of locations, by taking canoes up the river; these, finding him already in possession, applied to him for assistance in the way of food and drink, they being always, as he said, in total want. His first question always was, had they anything to pay for it with? On the reply being No, he told them, that if willing to work, he would supply them and enter their names in his book, at so much wages per day; that, he said, they were always glad to agree to.

He set them to work, and kept an account, giving them spirits and eatables, clothes, etc., getting them into his debt and keeping them to work it out, taking care to get their canoes into his possession, thus depriving them of their only means of escape from bondage.

By such devices he contrived to cut and raft a large quantity of timber each year. It was conveyed by stream to Montreal where he disposed of it; always laying out the proceeds – or the greater part – in some kind of stock or stores; thus, by degrees, he had reached the point of success and prosperity in which we found him. He was, at the time I speak of, nearly eighty years old: a healthy, active, little, old man, with hair as white as snow, and a quick grey eye; but, extraordinary to say, he had never thought of procuring a grant of the land he so unceremoniously invested himself with, until it was given him by Lord Dalhousie and the council, at that time at Quebec, and forming the Government of the province. With all his great property he told me he had no money, and that his business was carried on entirely by barter.

After spending a week with old Wright, we returned by the Ottawa river to St. Ann's, and thence proceeded by land to Montreal, where we were met by Lady Dalhousie, and took up quarters receiving, and giving parties to, the merchants of the north-west colony, and others in the neighbourhood of the town.

From thence to Sorel, where we remained for a few weeks, I, enjoying some extraordinary sport: shooting wild duck, woodcock, and snipe; of the latter my companion brought down, at one shot, nine birds, and we often shot from forty to fifty brace in a few hours, and without dogs. The woodcock I have often killed on the ground while feeding, being aware from the thickness of the bushes I could not get a shot at them on the wing.

Our winter at Quebec passed in the usual way without any particular incident. *So ended* 1820.

After the races of 1821 – at which I was again the winner – we started on a long tour, first to the Falls of Niagara, thence we proceeded to Lake Ontario.

Our party consisted of Lord Dalhousie, the quarter-master-general, another *aide-de-camp*, and myself.

At a small fort on the commencement of the lake were waiting to receive us, two well-equipped canoes, belonging to the North-Western Company – in charge of a gentleman of the company, a Mr. Shaw – each propelled by sixteen Canadian boatmen as paddlers, and a steersman, besides a guide for the lakes.[20]

The night before our embarkation we encamped at Fort Chippewee, and took our departure in the morning;[21] each person was supplied with a small mattress about a foot broad, which was rolled and put into an oilskin cover, serving as a seat in the canoe.

The party, including the boatmen, consisted in all of forty-four persons, which, with provisions for all and the baggage, was not a bad load for two boats, made of the bark of the birch, and in which not a nail was used.

Our destination in the first place was Detroit, a considerable town on the banks of the lake near the confines of Lake Huron. That place we reached the first day, and next morning we embarked, bag and baggage, canoes and all, on board an American sloop, in which we set sail for Drummond's Isles.[22]

There we found a garrison of one of the regiments, quartered at the time in Upper Canada. Some hundred Indians had arrived awaiting, by appointment, the arrival of the governor general to make speeches and receive presents.

We remained at Drummond's Isles for three days, thence we proceeded to a fort at the entrance to Lake Superior, which place, at the time, was occupied by a party of the North-Western Fur Company; from thence we entered Lake Superior, and, after proceeding some two or three days up the lake, returned by the same route to Drummond's Isles. The country, in my humble opinion, was anything but interesting, and the banks of the lakes low and covered with a thick jungle, where nothing was to be seen.

Altogether I thought it a most uncomfortable life, sitting squat-legged all day, and disembarking when the sun went down in a dreary waste to be devoured by mosquitos, which were in actual swarms; or, what was even worse, a small black fly that stung to such a degree that the faces of some of the party were so much swollen that you could not distinguish a feature. This might have been called pleasure by some persons, but not by me.

20 The North West Company was founded in 1779 to exploit the Canadian fur trade and rival the established Hudson's Bay Company. So bitter had this rivalry become by the time of Hay's sojourn in Canada, to the point that armed violence broke out on several occasions, that the two companies would be forcibly amalgamated in 1821 in order to end the competition.
21 Fort Chippawa, also known as Fort Welland, was constructed in 1791 to cover the portage road around the Niagara Falls. It changed hands several times during the War of 1812 but was abandoned by the military in the aftermath of that conflict.
22 Drummond Island, at the extremity of the Upper Peninsula of Michigan, was occupied by the British Army from 1815 to 1828, and a fort constructed there, before it was belatedly realised that the border agreement following the War of 1812 placed the site in American territory.

On leaving Drummond's Isles the second time, we proceeded to the entrance of what is called the French river, where we again embarked on board the canoes; and, after about ten days suffering, in the way I have described, arrived at a large bay from which the Ottawa, or Great River, as it is commonly called, takes its source.

At this point we were distant at least a thousand miles from an inhabited place, surrounded by immense forest trees and high rocky banks – beautifully wild scenery.

We began to disembark, unload, and pitch tents for the night, when I observed our conductor, Mr. Shaw, who had charge and responsibility of the whole expedition, looking very thoughtful and seemingly ill at ease; this, with him, was of rare occurrence, as he was of as light-hearted and happy a disposition as ever lived, and had long been accustomed to privations and dangers of every kind attendant on the wandering life of a north-west trader. Therefore, on seeing this change that had come over him, I feared he was ill.

But he soon undeceived me, by saying he wanted a little private conversation with me; then, taking me at a short distance from the party, he acquainted me with a circumstance that placed us all in a very unpleasant dilemma. It appeared the guide we had brought with us from Montreal – and who was the very best that could be obtained for the purpose of piloting the frail crafts in which we were journeying on the face of those mighty waters – was seriously ill from the great heat and exposure to the sun, and was, at this moment, in a state of delirium from brain fever. Our whole existence and the safety of the party depended on this man, as he alone knew all the rapids which we had to encounter on the course of the Ottawa.

At that point we were within eleven miles of some rapids down which we must descend in the morning, and not another man of the crew had ever navigated the river before.

Our provisions, which had been scanty for some time past, were nearly exhausted; indeed, the men had been for some days on the very short allowance of a small handful of Indian corn and a piece of suet, about the size of a nut, each day.

There was no portage by which we could convey the canoes, baggage, etc.; therefore the stream, with all its dangers, was our only resource, which simply meant taking our choice between being drowned or starved. Mr. Shaw's request to me was to make it known to his lordship, which I soon did; and a council of war was held by the party concerned, and we decided to take the chance of drowning on the passage down the Soalt [sic – Sault].

The next thing to be done was to select some one to guide the vessels down, as it must be done entirely by the eye; the stream running from fifty to sixty miles an hour between high rocks, the slightest touch on any of which would decide the fate of all on board.

The crews were assembled and the position of affairs explained to them, and all were asked if any one of them would undertake the pilotage of the canoes down the rapids, but not one could be found among the hardy Canadian boatmen that would undertake the perilous task. But amongst them was a young Indian lad of about eighteen who could not speak a word of any language but his native Indian; therefore Mr. Shaw was called upon to explain to him our situation, and to ask if he would undertake the task. Thomme did not hesitate, and undertook to guide us down, although never having seen the river before in his life.

That being settled, we returned to take our rest for the night, and in the morning, soon after daylight, again embarked, it was a most beautiful morning, the sun rising in all his splendour; every moment brought us nearer the point of danger; at last we arrived on the brink of the fall, or shute [sic], which extends, as I have described, far some miles; the roar of the water was deafening; the paddlers threw up their paddles and began to cross themselves.

The Indian, standing erect on the prow of the canoe, his long hair thrown back, the dead silence and anxiety on the faces of all, made it a striking picture.

Down we shot amongst foam and racks at an awful pace, about three or four minutes placed us once more so far in safety; the still stream at the bottom of the rapid was gained in about that short space, but not without a risk, as we had struck, fortunately, on a smooth surfaced rock had it been sharp or rugged I should not have been here now to relate the adventure.

This event so shook the nerves of Mr. Shaw that he made up his mind not to try the same game again, as the other rapids could be overcome by going round by portages and carrying the canoes and luggage, to which operations the boatmen are accustomed on their hardy expeditions, each man having a certain portion allotted to him, and three to each canoe – it is wonderful the burdens they carry.

There was still a difficulty to be overcome by us. It is the practice amongst themselves on such occasions, if one of their crew is taken ill and not able to help himself, to leave him behind to die a lingering death, every man having his portion of work so nicely divided that no one can be spared to assist the poor sick one, and life to them is of small value; but this arrangement we, of course, could not allow, and fortunately, from our provisions having been nearly exhausted and the burdens of those having to bear them being very light, a hand could be spared to carry the poor sufferer, which was done, causing a considerable delay and making the journey even more long and tedious.

The custom of these people was, as I have said, to leave their sick comrade to his fate, and then, on their next trip in that region, to visit the spot where he was left, and stick up a cross to his memory and bury his bones – if even they were left by the foxes and wolves that inhabit the wild forests of these parts.

After a most uncomfortable scramble by land and water and half-starved, we reached our friend Philemon Wright at the head of the Falls of the Ottawa, in about fourteen days from our starting from the source of the river. There, I must confess, I was right glad to find myself drawing towards something like civilised existence. We must have cut neat figures, our clothes in rags and our faces swollen to a shocking degree, with bites and stings of insects. However, these miseries were soon forgotten, and, after passing one night with our hosts, we proceeded onwards in the morning.

The next evening we had the satisfaction of hearing the boatmen singing Moore's well-known song, 'Row, brothers, row', in chorus, within sight and hearing of the church bells of St. Ann's, at which place we arrived about sundown, remaining at the inn all night.[23] Next day we started by road to Montreal, and I was glad our marches were brought to a close.

The remainder of the summer and autumn was spent in short excursions in the neighbourhood of Sorel, and, about October, we returned to the Castle of St. Lewis; there the winter of 1821 was spent as former ones.

At this time I was promoted to a troop of the 12th Dragoons, by purchase – after having been a subaltern for twelve years – which troop, being reduced to half-pay, the Duke of York, in the kindest way, gave in place of it a half-pay company of the 37th, by which I saved £1,300 of the purchase money.

In 1822, Lord Dalhousie proposed to pay a visit in the early summer, to Sir James Kempt, at that time Lieutenant-Governor of Nova Scotia; and proceeded there, returning to Quebec in the autumn of that year.[24]

I there heard of the death of my brother Alexander, in China, and I also received several letters, urging me earnestly to return home on leave. So, as I had, up to this time, been nearly fourteen years in the service, and, during that period, had never spent three months with my family, I mentioned to Lord Dalhousie, as he now had his nephew, the Hon. Fox Maule, to take my place as *aide-de-camp*, that I thought of going home, to which he agreed, as it was his intention to return himself in the spring of the next year. I, therefore, took leave of Canada; but was allowed to retain my staff appointment till Lord Dalhousie threw up his command.[25]

Some time towards the end of September, 1823, after a six years' sojourn in the North American Provinces, I took my passage in a homeward bound timber-laden vessel, with two or three other officers returning to England on leave of absence. Our voyage was a long and stormy one, being before the days in which steam navigation had been attempted as a mode of crossing the Atlantic Ocean. After various escapes from ice-bergs and the loss of masts by gales of wind, we were brought to anchor off Dover, when I soon found myself on English ground once more.

23   The song referred to is the 'Canadian Boat Song' composed in 1804 by the Irish poet Thomas Moore and based on earlier *voyageur* songs.

24   Lt. General Sir James Kempt was a veteran of the Peninsula, the War of 1812, and of Waterloo. He served as Lieutenant Governor of Nova Scotia 1820-1828, and then succeeded Dalhousie as Governor General of British North America 1828-1830.

25   Maule, after a short military career, became a politician and is better known as Lord Panmure, the title to which he succeeded in 1852. He served as Secretary of State for War during the Crimean War and in 1860 succeeded to the Dalhousie Earldom.

5

Home Service 1824-1828[1]

Having delivered my despatches at the Horse Guards to the Military Secretary, at that time Sir Herbert Taylor, he offered me a company on full-pay, which I foolishly refused, wishing to again return to cavalry – more easily wished for than accomplished.[2]

I then proceeded to Scotland, but, after a few weeks at home, I proposed to my father to allow me once more to make an attempt to get back to a regiment of cavalry, and resume my military life. He, who was always anxious to meet my wishes, gave his consent, and, in the spring of 1824, I took my departure for London to see what could be done at the Horse Guards.

After some weeks spent in the great metropolis I succeeded in effecting an exchange to full-pay in the 5th Dragoon Guards with an old acquaintance of my own, a Captain Christie, I gave him a difference between full- and half-pay of £2,200, and, as soon as I had made my arrangements, I returned to Spott to make preparations for my final departure to join my new corps, at the time quartered at Dundalk in Ireland; and, having purchased a horse, equipments, etc., I proceeded thence.[3] In Ireland I remained till the next spring, 1825, when the regiment moved quarters to Glasgow, where I fully enjoyed the hospitality of the whole neighbourhood, seldom having the pleasure of dining one day in seven at the mess.

From Glasgow, in the autumn, I was sent to command the squadron quartered at Hamilton; while there I received great kindness from the Duke of Hamilton, Lord Dalhousie, Lord Buchan, and others.

---

1   This chapter was originally presented as Part III of the work.
2   Lt. General Sir Herbert Taylor had served most of his military career as a courtier and diplomat, interspersed with a brief but distinguished stint as a brigadier under Graham in Flanders 1813-1814. He held the office of Military Secretary 1820-1827.
3   The exchange between Captain William Hay, half-pay 37th Foot, and Captain Braithwaite Christie, 5th Dragoon Guards, took place on 1 July 1824 and was recorded in the London Gazette of the 10th of that month (Issue 18043, p.1131). Strangely, the title of this section in the original edition of the memoir gives Hay's new regiment as the 5th Light Dragoons, a non-existent corps.

'The 5th Dragoon Guards' Aquatint after William Heath, 1828.
(Anne S.K. Brown Military Collection)

In the spring of 1826, we marched to Newcastle – the headquarters of the regiment being sent to York. After spending a very pleasant time there, my troop was ordered to Carlisle to quell riots, etc.

There we spent the winter of 1826, a great deal of the time most happily, with Sir. T. Maxwell, of Spring Keld, from whose hospitable house myself, in company with Streatfield, got back one very cold winter's night sometime between the hours of 12 and 2 a.m.[4] I had tumbled into bed, and had hardly composed myself to sleep, when the door was suddenly opened, my servant and the troop sergeant-major presenting themselves to my astonished sight, the latter with a big letter in his hand, with the ominous words on the back: 'Immediate Service, Horse Guards, London'. This was nothing more or less than an order to march immediately with the troop, by forced marches to Sheffield, at which place riots were apprehended; and there to report my arrival to the officer commanding the district, at that time Sir J. Byng, the present Lord Strafford.[5]

This meant a most unpleasant and difficult march for a dragoon regiment, as enough snow had fallen to make the roads a sheet of ice, and the frost was very hard and the air intensely cold; however, march we did, and, on reaching the Cumberland Hills – the second day – we quartered at a place called Bruffs.[6] Here, seeing the state of the weather and to avoid the danger of delay, I determined to cheat a snowstorm at such inhospitable quarters; to do this I was obliged to lead my men, though with the greatest difficulty, in a forced night march, and glad I was that I did so, as by the next morning the snow had fallen and drifted on the road to such a depth that the regiment following mine (the 9th Dragoons [sic – Lancers]) were obliged to remain three weeks in Cumberland before proceeding.

Difficult as the march was, I was amply repaid when I reached the sunshiny banks looking down on Barnard Castle, and was congratulated upon my masterly move, receiving the approbation of the general for the decided step I had taken in extricating my men and bringing them, in so short a time, to Sheffield, and in such good order.

Here, with Streatfield and others, I enjoyed hunting to my heart's content, being in the centre of four different crack packs of hounds.

Towards the summer I re-joined the headquarters of the regiment at Leeds, where we spent the winter of 1827. Nearing the spring I was taken very ill, and was recommended to proceed to London for advice; there I had to lie up for at least two months; but, under the skilful treatment of our kind friend Dr. J. Wardrop, I got

4   Hay's companion was Lt. Richard Shuttleworth Streatfield, 5th Dragoon Guards.
5   Lt. General Sir John Byng, who had commanded the 2nd Brigade at Waterloo and would be created Baron Strafford in 1835, was then General Officer Commanding the Northern District.
6   Location in fact Brough, Cumbria. Hay's route across the Pennines was via Stainmore along the line of the modern A66, a passage which, even today, is subject to being blocked by inclement weather.

on my legs once more, and took my departure to pay the last visit I ever made to my native home Spott.

In the autumn I again joined my regiment at Dorchester, where, as at most country quarters, we led a dull life; but the most important event of mine, I suppose, was predestined to take place there.

For want of a pastime, I kept a lot of greyhounds, and, by the kindness of the neighbouring landed proprietors, we had leave to course; and at the house of one of these gentlemen, in the neighbourhood of Dorchester, I met, on one of the coursing days, the lady who, a few months later, became my wife – your dear mother.[7]

At the urgent desire of my father-in-law I now left the Army, and, after living about two years in Surrey and seven in Scotland, I came to London, and received the appointment of Inspecting-Superintendent, and later on that of Commissioner, of the Metropolitan Police.[8]

CAPTAIN WILLIAM HAY

RECEIVED THE ORDER OF COMPANION OF THE BATH FOR

SERVICES DURING THE EXHIBITION OF 1851.

HE ALSO, AND WHICH HE VALUED MORE HIGHLY,

HAD MEDALS (WITH CLASPS) FOR

THE PENINSULA AND WATERLOO.

HE DIED, MUCH BELOVED AND REGRETTED IN THE

FORCE TO WHICH HIS LAST YEARS HAD BEEN GIVEN

ON AUGUST 29, 1855; AGED 63

7   Hay's bride was Sarah Sparkes, daughter of Richard Sparkes of Dorchester.
8   The *London Gazette* of 15 December 1829 (Issue 18637, p.2326) notes the promotion of 'Lieutenant John Lewis Hampton to be Captain, by purchase, vice Hay, who retires', the transaction being dated 12 November of that year.

Appendix

List of Engagements Etc.

1810		
Oct. 10	Sobral	Near Torres Vedras

(The two magnificent lines of defence, constructed by Wellington at Torres Vedras, with Sobral as the central redoubt, arrested the French advance, and their permanent retreat commenced from this spot.)

1811		
March 11	Pombal[1]	Affair
" 12	Redinha	"
" 13	Condacia	"
" 14	Cazal Nova	"
" 15	Fez de Aronce	"
April 3	Sabugal	Battle
May 3	Near Fort Conception	Affair
" 5	Fuentes d'Onore	Battle
" 6	"	"
Sept. 26	Guinaldo	Affair
	Investment of Ciudad Rodrigo	

The above with the 52nd Light Infantry.
The following with the 12th Light Dragoons.

1812		
Nov. 6	Retreat from Burgos	
" 8	Heights of St. Christoval	Affair
" 14	Passage of the Tormes	"
" 16	Huebro	Affairs for three days[2]

1813		
May 30	Esla	Skirmish
June 11	Hormaza	"
" 18	Osma	"
" 21	Vittoria	Battle
" 23	Toulouse[3]	Skirmish
	Pyrenees, say, 5	"
Oct. 6	Passage of the Biddasoa [sic] River	
Nov. 10	Nivelle	Skirmish[4]
Dec. 10	St. Jean de Luz	"
" 11	Campo[5]	
" 13	Nive	Battle
	Vincentes, at least, say, 4[6]	Affairs
" 15	Passage of the Adour	Skirmish
	At Dax	"
1814		
March	Paulliac near Bordeaux[7]	"
	On the Staff of Lord Dalhousie	

1815
June 16, 17, and 18, Waterloo and Others – three Battles.

Notes
1   For the identification of the May 1811 actions, and their locations, see p.24, fn.21.
2   The skirmishing on the Huebra at the conclusion of the Burgos retreat.
3   Not the city in France but Tolosa, in northern Spain, where fighting took place during the pursuit of the French after Vitoria.
4   A classification that presumably reflects how lightly the 12th Light Dragoons were actually engaged in what was in fact a major battle.
5   Cambo-les-Bains, on the River Nive 12 miles south-east of Bayonne.
6   In the aftermath of the Battles of the Nive and St Pierre, the 12th Light Dragoons were part of a cavalry force shifted to meet a thrust against Wellington's right-rear by detached French forces. The resultant clash took place around Cambo-les-Bains and Hasparren, and it is quite possible that the earlier mention of the former place is out of sequence and is what is actually meant here. Hay's 'Vincentes' cannot be located.
7   Presumably the skirmishing in which Hay claims to have foiled the plot to ambush the duc d'Angoulême. The action at Étauliers, which one might expect to see listed as well, took place in April.

Index

Please note that people and places are indexed under their correct names, as per the spelling used in the editorial notes, rather than following Hay's original miss-spellings.

From Reason to Revolution series – Warfare c 1721-1815

http://www.helion.co.uk/published-by-helion/reason-to-revolution-1721-1815.html

The 'From Reason to Revolution' series covers the period of military history c. 1721–1815, an era in which fortress-based strategy and linear battles gave way to the nation-in-arms and the beginnings of total war.

This era saw the evolution and growth of light troops of all arms, and of increasingly flexible command systems to cope with the growing armies fielded by nations able to mobilise far greater proportions of their manpower than ever before. Many of these developments were fired by the great political upheavals of the era, with revolutions in America and France bringing about social change which in turn fed back into the military sphere as whole nations readied themselves for war. Only in the closing years of the period, as the reactionary powers began to regain the upper hand, did a military synthesis of the best of the old and the new become possible.

The series will examine the military and naval history of the period in a greater degree of detail than has hitherto been attempted, and has a very wide brief, with the intention of covering all aspects from the battles, campaigns, logistics, and tactics, to the personalities, armies, uniforms, and equipment.

Submissions

The publishers would be pleased to receive submissions for this series. Please contact us via email (andrewbamford18@gmail.com), or in writing to Helion & Company Limited, 26 Willow Road, Solihull, West Midlands, B91 1UE.

Titles

No 1 *Lobositz to Leuthen. Horace St Paul and the Campaigns of the Austrian Army in the Seven Years War 1756-57* Translated with additional materials by Neil Cogswell (ISBN 978-1-911096-67-2)

No 2 *Glories to Useless Heroism. The Seven Years' War in North America from the French journals of Comte Maurès de Malartic, 1755-1760* William Raffle (ISBN 978-1-911512-19-6) (paperback)

No 3 *Reminiscences 1808-1815 under Wellington. The Peninsular and Waterloo Memoirs of William Hay* William Hay, with notes and commentary by Andrew Bamford (ISBN 978-1-911512-32-5)

No 4 *Far Distant Ships. The Blockade of Brest 1793-1815* Quintin Barry (ISBN 978-1-911512-14-1)

Books within the series are published in two formats: 'Falconets' are paperbacks, page size 248mm × 180mm, with high visual content including colour plates; 'Culverins' are hardback monographs, page size 234mm × 156mm. Books marked with * in the list above are Falconets, all others are Culverins unless otherwise noted.